GETTYSBURG

THE GETTYSBURG ADDRESS
ꞏXIX NOVEMBER ꞏ MDCCCLXIII ꞏ

☆

FOURSCORE & SEVEN YEARS AGO OUR FATHERS BROUGHT FORTH ON THIS CONTINENT A NEW NATION ꞏ CONCEIVED IN LIBERTY ꞏ AND DEDICATED TO THE PROPOSITION THAT ALL MEN ARE CREATED EQUAL ꞏ

NOW WE ARE ENGAGED IN A GREAT CIVIL WAR ꞏ TESTING WHETHER THAT NATION ꞏ OR ANY NATION SO CONCEIVED AND SO DEDICATED ꞏ CAN LONG ENDURE ꞏ WE ARE MET ON A GREAT BATTLE-FIELD OF THAT WAR ꞏ WE HAVE COME TO DEDICATE A PORTION OF THAT FIELD AS A FINAL RESTING PLĀCE FOR THOSE WHO HERE GAVE THEIR LIVES THAT THAT NATION MIGHT LIVE ꞏ IT IS ALTOGETHER FITTING & PROPER THAT WE SHOULD DO THIS ꞏ

BUT ꞏ IN LARGER SENSE ꞏ WE CANNOT DEDICATE—WE CANNOT CONSECRATE—WE CANNOT HALLOW—THIS GROUND ꞏ THE BRAVE MEN ꞏ LIVING AND DEAD ꞏ WHO STRUGGLED HERE HAVE CONSECRATED IT FAR ABOVE OUR POOR POWER TO ADD OR DETRACT ꞏ THE WORLD WILL LITTLE NOTE NOR LONG REMEMBER WHAT WE SAY HERE ꞏ BUT IT CAN NEVER FORGET WHAT THEY DID HERE ꞏ IT IS FOR US ꞏ THE LIVING ꞏ RATHER ꞏ TO BE DEDICATED HERE TO THE UNFINISHED WORK WHICH THEY WHO FOUGHT HERE HAVE THUS FAR SO NOBLY ADVANCED ꞏ IT IS RATHER FOR US TO BE HERE DEDICATED TO THE GREAT TASK REMAINING BEFORE US—THAT FROM THESE HONORED DEAD WE TAKE INCREASED DEVOTION TO THAT CAUSE FOR WHICH THEY GAVE THE LAST FULL MEASURE OF DEVOTION ꞏ THAT WE HERE HIGHLY RESOLVE THAT THESE DEAD SHALL NOT HAVE DIED IN VAIN ꞏ THAT THIS NATION ꞏ UNDER GOD ꞏ SHALL HAVE A NEW BIRTH OF FREEDOM ꞏ AND THAT GOVERNMENT OF THE PEOPLE ꞏ BY THE PEOPLE ꞏ FOR THE PEOPLE ꞏ SHALL NOT PERISH FROM THE EARTH ꞏ

ꞏ ABRAHAM LINCOLN ꞏ

GETTYSBURG

THE PLACE
THE BATTLES
THE OUTCOME

By W. C. STORRICK

BARNES
&NOBLE
BOOKS
NEW YORK

This edition published by Barnes & Noble, Inc.

1993 Barnes & Noble Books

ISBN 1-56619-032-0

Printed and bound in the United States of America

M 9 8 7 6 5 4 3 2

INTRODUCTION

THE LITERATURE of the Battle of Gettysburg is enormous in volume. Not only do general histories of the Civil War devote many pages to an analysis of its strategy, but many separate volumes enumerate each maneuver, however small, discuss moot points, assign praise for victory or blame for defeat, and describe the personnel of the commanders. Most of these works are valuable to the historian but not interesting to the average visitor to the field who wishes a description of the contest reduced to simplest terms, a selection of the romantic and dramatic incidents which abound, and an account of the extensive cemetery and park.

Mr. Storrick's book satisfies these requirements. Born a short distance from the field, he remembers the flight from home as the troops advanced. He heard Lincoln deliver his immortal address, and he has been a constant student of the battle and its field. He is probably better informed upon both subjects than any other living man. For more than twenty years he was connected with the Battlefield Commission, in charge of much of its territory, and in later years he has been the Superintendent of Guides. In the office and on the field he has encountered many great men—hundreds of officers and

privates, both Union and Confederate, who fought the battle; sculptors — Bush-Brown, Sievers, and Borglum—who have come to select sites for their works or to see them unveiled; presidents of the United States and their families; generations of West Point students, and historians, statesmen, and military men from this and other lands.

Frequently called upon to guide visitors over the field, to explain the relief map, and to give information about some obscure point, Mr. Storrick has in this volume reduced the story of the battle to its simplest elements. It is obviously impossible to describe a complicated military engagement as one would tell of a walk or a drive, but Mr. Storrick's account should be easily understood by all but the very young. It surely places before the visitor what he needs to know in order to comprehend the importance of this epochal contest. The stories of minor incidents are no less authentic than the account of the battle, and they add the personal touch.

ELSIE SINGMASTER LEWARS

CONTENTS

7

CONTENTS

GETTYSBURG

CHAPTER I

BEFORE THE BATTLE

T O TELL the story of a great battle without impeding the sweep of events with too much detail is a difficult matter. Too many incidents and interesting sidelights divert attention from the main narrative. Nevertheless sufficient detail must be presented to make the movements clear, and to enable students to understand the tactical situation.

If the visitor is not satisfied with the brief outline here presented, he is recommended to read further in the books listed, and especially to employ a guide, without whose trained and supervised services the best manual is inadequate. The reader in search of romance is recommended to the successive INCIDENTS OF THE BATTLE as herein presented.

According to official records, the Gettysburg campaign of 1863 began on June 3rd and ended on August 1st. No effort will be made to describe the movements, counter-movements, and fifty minor engagements that occurred before the armies crossed the Mason and Dixon's line

and finally concentrated at Gettysburg, where they engaged in battle on July 1st, 2nd, and 3rd. It is necessary, however, that the visitor should understand the approach to the field.

LOCATION OF THE ARMIES On June 3rd the Union Army, called the Army of the Potomac, lay at Falmouth, Va., on the north side of the Rappahannock River, Major-General Joseph Hooker in command.

The Confederate Army, called the Army of Northern Virginia, occupied the south bank, with headquarters at Fredericksburg, General Robert E. Lee in command.

Both armies were resting after the major engagement at Chancellorsville, in which the Confederates were victorious.

The Army of the Potomac was made up of seven infantry and one cavalry corps. It numbered at the time of the battle approximately 84,000.

The Army of Northern Virginia was made up of three infantry corps and one division of cavalry. It numbered at the time of the battle about 75,000.

Following the text is a roster of officers, which should be consulted, both for an understanding of the battle and because of the obligation to honor brave men.

GENERAL LEE'S PLAN During the month of May, General Lee visited Richmond to discuss with the Confederate government various plans involving political

and military considerations. Up to this time, the South had won the major victories, but her resources, both in men and sinews of war, were diminishing, and a prolonged conflict would be disastrous. It was decided that the army should invade the North via the Shenandoah and Cumberland valleys, with Harrisburg as an objective. This route not only afforded a continuous highway but put the army in a position to threaten Baltimore, Philadelphia, and Washington from the north. The Blue Ridge Mountains to the east would screen the advance, and the rich agricultural section would furnish supplies of food and forage.

The time was propitious. General Lee's army was in the prime of condition. The North was discouraged by losses, distrustful of Lincoln, weary of war. The South believed that one great victory would assure her the friendliness of the leading powers of Europe. Her independence once acknowledged, she could import the materials of war and the necessities of life which she lacked. It was thought certain that at the prospect of invasion the North would withdraw troops from the siege of Vicksburg then being conducted by General Grant. With high hopes the march was begun.

On June 3rd Lee put his army in motion LEE'S FIRST northward, with Ewell's Corps, preceded by MOVEMENT Jenkins' and Imboden's Cavalry, in the advance,

followed by Longstreet and lastly by Hill. Longstreet moved on the east side of the Blue Ridge in order to lead Hooker to believe that Washington would be threatened. On reaching Snicker's Gap, he crossed the Ridge into the Shenandoah Valley and followed Hill, who was now in advance. The great army was strung out from Fredericksburg, Va., on the south to Martinsburg, W. Va., on the north, with the cavalry division under Stuart guarding the gaps along the Blue Ridge.

After driving out Union forces stationed at Winchester under Milroy, Lee's Army crossed the Potomac at Williamsport and Shepherdstown on June 23rd, 24th, and 25th, and advanced northward, unopposed, through the Cumberland Valley, toward Harrisburg.

HOOKER'S
PLAN

On June 10th, Hooker proposed to President Lincoln that he cross the Rappahannock and attack Hill, who still remained, and then move south, threatening Richmond. He thought this might divert Lee from his invasion of the North. In reply Lincoln said:

"I think Lee's Army and not Richmond is your sure objective point."

APPOINT-
MENT OF
MEADE

Thereupon Hooker started in pursuit of Lee on June 13th, moving east of the Blue Ridge on a line parallel with Lee on the west, with the cavalry guarding his left. He thus protected

Baltimore and Washington. He crossed the Potomac at Edward's Ferry on the 25th and 26th and reached Frederick on the 27th, where he halted. Believing himself handicapped by orders from General Halleck, Chief in Command at Washington, who refused the use of the Union forces at Harper's Ferry, he asked to be relieved of the command of the Army of the Potomac. The request was granted, and, on June 28th, Major-General George G. Meade, in command of the 5th Corps, was appointed his successor, Sykes taking command of General Meade's Corps.

Lee's Army had been steadily moving north- ward in the Cumberland Valley. Ewell, in the advance, detached Early's Division on reaching Chambersburg, directing him to move through Gettysburg on June 26th and thence to York and Wrightsville, there to cross the Susquehanna to Columbia and move up to Harrisburg to meet the divisions of Rodes and Johnson. Rodes reached Carlisle on June 28th, accompanied by Ewell; Johnson was at Greenvillage, between Chambersburg and Carlisle. Hill moved from Chambersburg to Cashtown, and Longstreet was in the rear at Chambersburg. Lee's head- quarters were in Messersmith's Woods near Chambersburg.

In his advance into Gettysburg, Early was opposed by the 26th Emergency Regiment of

ADVANCE OF LEE

Pennsylvania Volunteers, Company A consisting of students of Pennsylvania (now Gettysburg) College, citizens of the town, and some volunteers from Harrisburg. After skirmishing on the Chambersburg Pike about 3 miles from the town, this regiment was obliged to retreat, finally reaching Harrisburg. About 175 were captured, but were afterward paroled. On the same day, George Sandoe, a Union scout, was shot by one of Early's pickets on the Baltimore Pike. He was the first Union soldier killed in the vicinity of Gettysburg prior to the battle.

On account of the absence of his cavalry under Stuart, who had been left with five brigades to guard the rear and hold the gaps of the Blue Ridge, Lee did not know until June 28th that the Union Army had crossed the Potomac and was threatening his line of communication with the South. Learning this he ordered a concentration of his forces at Cashtown.

MEADE'S MOVEMENT On assuming command, General Meade moved his army northward from the vicinity of Frederick and established a tentative line along Pipe Creek, between Manchester on his right and Emmitsburg on his left, with headquarters near Taneytown.

STUART'S MOVEMENT After the Union Army crossed the Potomac, Stuart left the line of the Blue Ridge with three brigades of cavalry and made a raid around the

Union Army, crossing the Potomac at Seneca Creek and moving thence to Hanover, where he engaged Kilpatrick's Division of Union cavalry on June 30th. Passing through Jefferson, Dover, and Dillsburg to Carlisle, he reached Carlisle on the afternoon of July 1st, getting into communication with Lee, after an interval of a week.

On June 30th, Pender's Division, Hill's Corps, moved from Fayetteville to Cashtown; Anderson's Division to Fayetteville; Rodes' Division, Ewell's Corps, from Carlisle via Petersburg to Heidlersburg. Early's Division advanced from York through Weiglestown and East Berlin, and encamped 3 miles from Heidlersburg. Johnson's Division marched from Greenvillage to Scotland. Hood's and McLaws' Divisions, Longstreet's Corps, moved from Chambersburg to Fayetteville; Pickett's Division remained at Chambersburg. Lee's headquarters were at Greenwood. SITUATION OF CONFEDERATE FORCES ON JUNE 30TH

On June 30th the 11th Corps was at Emmitsburg, the 1st at Marsh Creek, the 3rd at Bridgeport, the 5th at Union Mills, the 6th at Manchester, the 12th at Littlestown, the 2nd at Taneytown. Two brigades of Buford's Cavalry Division were at Gettysburg; Gregg's Cavalry Division was at Manchester; Kilpatrick's at Hanover. Meade's headquarters were established at Taneytown, twelve miles south of Gettysburg. SITUATION OF UNION FORCES ON JUNE 30TH

15

Neither commander yet foresaw Gettysburg as a field of battle. Each had expected to take a strong position and force his adversary to attack. But in the hot summer weather fate was moving the mighty hosts closer and closer. The sky was cloudless, and the summer moon was at its brightest. The wheat was ripe, and the armies marched between partly reaped fields.

On the 30th, Hill, in the front at Cashtown, sent Pettigrew's Brigade to Gettysburg for supplies, shoes especially being badly needed. In the meantime, Meade ordered Buford, with two brigades of cavalry at Emmitsburg, to make a reconnaissance to Gettysburg. Buford reported:

> "I entered this place today at 11 A.M. Found everybody in a terrible state of excitement on account of the enemy's advance."

On reaching Seminary Ridge, Pettigrew saw the approach of Buford. Not wishing to bring on an engagement, he withdrew to the vicinity of Cashtown.

Buford moved through the town and bivouacked for the night west of the Seminary, along McPherson Ridge. He assigned to Gamble's Brigade the task of watching the Fairfield and Cashtown roads and to Devin the Mummasburg, Middletown (now Biglerville), and Harrisburg roads. Early on the morning of the 1st, he picketed all the roads leading north and northeast.

General Meade's Statue. General Meade viewed Pickett's Charge from the center of the Union line. This statue, like those of Reynolds and Sedgwick, is the work of Henry K. Bush-Brown

The Virginia Memorial. The bronze group represents the various arms of the Confederate service. Above is a portrait statue of General Lee. The Memorial is the work of F. W. Sievers.

MAJOR-GENERAL GEORGE GORDON MEADE

George Gordon Meade was born on December 30, 1815, in Cadiz, Spain, where his father was an agent of the United States Navy. He was graduated at West Point in 1835, and, after serving one year in the army, resigned to begin practice as a civil engineer. He was frequently employed by the Government and re-entered military service in 1842. He served with distinction on the staffs of Taylor and Scott in the Mexican War. At the outbreak of the Civil War he was placed in command of a brigade of volunteers, soon rising to the command of a division and joining his fortunes permanently to those of the Army of the Potomac. He led his division through the Seven Days' Battle, being severely wounded at Glendale. He served through the Antietam campaign and at Fredericksburg, where he particularly distinguished himself. At Chancellorsville he commanded the 5th Corps. When Hooker resigned the command of the army, and while the army was en route to check Lee's invasion of the North, he was appointed Hooker's successor. He accepted the command with reluctance and from a sense of duty. At Gettysburg he won undying fame as an able military leader.

When General Grant assumed command of the Armies of the North in 1864, Meade continued in command of the Army of the Potomac with a mutual good feeling which enabled them to maintain this relation throughout the war. At the close of the war, Meade commanded the military division of the Atlantic until his death, November 6, 1872.

CORPS BADGES OF THE FEDERAL ARMY

1st Corps—Full Moon.	6th Corps—Greek Cross.
2d Corps—Trefoil.	11th Corps—Crescent.
3d Corps—Diamond.	12th Corps—Five-Pointed Star.
5th Corps—Cross of Malta.	

Badges always in Red for 1st Division; White, for 2nd; Blue, for 3rd.
The corps badges appear upon all regimental monuments upon the battlefield. The Confederate Army had no corps badges.

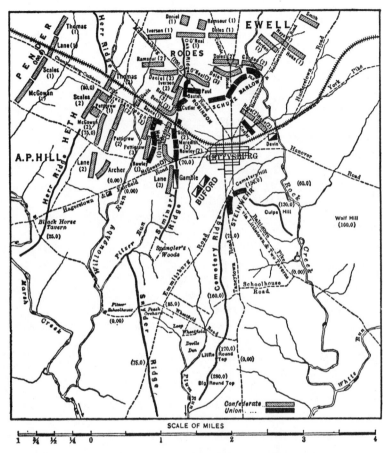

Position of the First Day's Battle

(Gettysburg is the county seat of Adams County, Pennsylvania. It is 37 miles (by highway) from Harrisburg on the northeast, 29 miles from York (on the Lincoln Highway) eastward. Pittsburgh is 179 miles westward and Baltimore 53 miles southward. See also page 138.)

18

CHAPTER II

THE FIRST DAY'S BATTLE

HILL learned from Pettigrew that Union forces had reached Gettysburg, and anxious to know their strength, he sent Heth's and Pender's Divisions with Pegram's battalion of artillery forward on a reconnaissance in force. This movement, made at 5.30 A.M. on July 1, precipitated the battle.

The advance was soon interrupted by Buford's skirmishers. On reaching Herr Ridge, which crosses the Cashtown Road at right angles, Hill deployed his line of battle—Heth on both sides of the road with Pender in reserve. Pegram posted his artillery on Herr Ridge, and at 8 o'clock fired his first shot. Buford's artillery, under Calef, posted on the opposite ridge, fired in reply. The battle was on, and the gravity of the situation was clear to Buford, who at 10.10 A.M. sent this message to Meade:

> "The enemy's force are advancing on me at this point and driving my pickets and skirmishers very rapidly. There is a large force at Heidlersburg that is driving my pickets at that point from that direction. I am sure that the whole of A. P. Hill's force is advancing."

Union reinforcements were at hand. General ARRIVAL OF Reynolds, in advance of the 1st Corps, arrived REYNOLDS from Marsh Creek, via the Emmitsburg Road.

After a short conference with Buford at the Seminary buildings, he sent an orderly urging Wadsworth, whose division was advancing across the fields, to hasten. On its arrival, Reynolds posted Cutler to the right, across the railroad cut which lies parallel to the Chambersburg Pike, and Meredith on the left. (Reynolds Avenue now marks this line.)

DEATH OF
REYNOLDS After posting Hall's battery in place of Calef's, Reynolds rode to the McPherson Woods, and while directing the advance of Meredith at 10.15 A.M. was instantly killed by a Confederate sharpshooter. Doubleday consequently assumed command of the 1st Corps, and Rowley succeeded Doubleday in command of the Division. Compelled to fall back into the grove, Buford moved his cavalry to the left near the Fairfield Road, and Meredith advanced into the woods, drove Hill's right across Willoughby Run, and captured General Archer and part of his men.

On the Union right, Cutler was attacked in flank by Davis's Brigade, of the left of Hill's line, and was compelled to withdraw. Davis advanced into the railroad cut where part of his force was captured. He then withdrew to his original line.

A MORNING
LULL At 11 A.M. there was a lull. Doubleday withdrew his forces from across Willoughby Run and established a new line through the McPherson Woods from north to south. Robinson's Division

reached the field and was held in reserve at the Seminary buildings. Rowley's Division (formerly Doubleday's) arrived a little later; Stone's Brigade of this Division was deployed in the front line on what is now Stone Avenue, and Biddle's Brigade was placed on the left of Meredith, along what is now South Reynolds Avenue. In the afternoon, Robinson's Division was moved to the right, prolonging the Union line to the Mummasburg Road in order to meet the advance of Rodes' Division, coming forward via the Carlisle Road. Devin's cavalry was moved from Buford's right to the vicinity of the York Pike and the Hanover Road.

In this preliminary action of the forenoon the advantage was in favor of the Union forces. The Confederate General Heth reported:

"The enemy had now been felt, and found in heavy force in and around Gettysburg. The division was now formed in line of battle on the right of the road; Archer's brigade on the right, Pettigrew's in the center, and Brockenbrough's on the left. Davis's brigade was kept on the left of the road that it might collect its stragglers, and from its shattered condition it was not deemed advisable to bring it again into action that day."

The Union General Buford reported:

"On July 1, between 8 and 9 A.M. reports came in from the 1st Brigade (Colonel Gamble's) that the enemy was coming down from toward Cashtown in force. Colonel Gamble made an admirable line of battle,

and moved off proudly to meet him. The two lines soon became hotly engaged, we having the advantage of position, he of numbers. The 1st Brigade held its own for more than two hours, and had to be literally dragged back a few hundred yards to a more secure and sheltered position."

ARRIVAL OF RODES AND EARLY — On learning at Middletown (now Biglerville) that Hill was engaged with the Union forces at Gettysburg, Rodes marched thither directly via the Carlisle Road. Early approached via the Harrisburg or Heidlersburg Road. The advance of both was quickened by the sound of cannonading. Arriving a little past noon, Rodes deployed his Division of five brigades on both sides of Oak Ridge, his right on the left of Heth's Division and his left with Early's right, extending across the plain north of the town. Carter's artillery was posted on Oak Hill.

THE OPPOSING LINES — Robinson's Division of the 1st Union Corps was moved from its position in reserve at the Seminary buildings to the right of Cutler, to oppose Rodes' Confederate line.

Hill prolonged his right by bringing up Pender's Division that had been held in reserve. The artillery of McIntosh's battalion was brought into action in support. These guns, with Carter's and Pegram's, together numbering 60, and 11 brigades of infantry now opposed the much smaller 1st Union Corps of only 36 guns and 6 brigades.

General Howard, in command of the 11th Union Corps, reached Gettysburg from Emmitsburg between 10 and 11 A.M., in advance of his Corps, and took command of the Union forces. Schurz succeeded Howard in command of the Corps, and Doubleday resumed command of his Division.

On reaching Gettysburg, Howard went to the top of the Fahnestock building at the corner of Baltimore and Middle streets to observe the lines of battle. He reported:

"I had studied the position a few moments, when a report reached me that General Reynolds was wounded. At first I hoped his wound might be slight and that he would continue to command, but in a short time I was undeceived. His aid-de-camp, Major William Riddle, brought the sad tidings of his death. This was about 11.30 A.M. Prior to this the General had sent me orders to move up at a double quick, for he was severely engaged. On hearing of the death of Reynolds, I assumed command of the left wing, instructing General Schurz to take command of the 11th Corps. After an examination of the general features of the country, I came to the conclusion that the only tenable position for my limited force was the ridge to the southeast of Gettysburg (now well known as Cemetery Ridge). I at once established my headquarters near the cemetery, and on the highest point north of the Baltimore Pike."

On the arrival of the 11th Corps, Howard ordered Schurz to move the 3rd and 1st Divisions to positions north of the town, while the 2nd Division was held on Cemetery Hill in reserve.

On account of the prior arrival of the Confederates under Rodes, who covered the plain north of the town, Schurz was unable to connect with the right of the Union left on Oak Hill, and a gap remained between the two lines. The position of the 11th Corps coincides with what is now Howard Avenue.

THE CONFEDERATE GENERAL EARLY'S POSITION

Shortly after the 11th Corps moved to the front, Early's Division of Ewell's Corps arrived from Heidlersburg and went into line to the right of Howard, connecting with Rodes' left across the plain. Early posted his artillery, Jones's battalion, in position to enfilade the right of Howard, while Carter's batteries on Oak Hill enfiladed the left. The Confederate forces largely exceeded the Union forces, the former being about 28,000 and the latter about 18,000. The whole Confederate line advanced and attacked the Union forces in front and on both flanks. On Oak Hill part of Rodes' forces, O'Neal's and Iverson's brigades, were repulsed, a large part of the latter being captured.

THE UNION RETREAT

After a strenuous resistance the whole Union line was compelled to withdraw to Cemetery Hill. The 11th Corps retreated through the center of town where many were captured. The 1st Corps fell back through the western part of the town. By 4.30 P.M. all the territory held by the Union forces was occupied by the Confederates.

General Lee reached the field from Cashtown ARRIVAL OF about 3 P.M., witnessed the retreat of the Union LEE forces, and established his headquarters in tents in an apple orchard back of the Seminary. He ordered Ewell to follow up the repulse if he thought it practicable. In this connection Ewell reported:

"The enemy had fallen back to a commanding position known as Cemetery Hill, south of Gettysburg, and quickly showed a formidable front there. On entering the town, I received a message from the Commanding General to attack this hill, if I could do so to advantage. I could not bring artillery to bear on it, and all the troops with me were jaded by twelve hours' marching and fighting, and I was notified that General Johnson's division (the only one of my corps that had not been engaged) was close to town. Cemetery Hill was not assailable from the town. . . . Before Johnson could be placed in position the night was far advanced."

General Hill reported:

"Under the impression that the enemy was entirely routed, my own two divisions exhausted by some six hours' hard fighting, prudence led me to be content with what had been gained."

The failure of Ewell to follow up the repulse and capture Cemetery Hill and Culp's Hill, defended by a weak line of the Union forces, enabled the Union commanders to establish during the night a line of defence that was secure against attack. By many military critics, this is generally considered Lee's lost opportunity.

The retreating Union soldiers were met at East Cemetery Hill by Generals Hancock and Howard, who directed them to positions, the 1st Corps on Cemetery Ridge and Culp's Hill, and the 11th on East Cemetery Hill. The 12th Corps arrived on the Baltimore Pike, and soon after Sickles' 3rd Corps came up from Emmitsburg.

Hancock had been instructed by Meade to take command and report if he thought the ground a suitable place to continue the battle. A battle-line was at once established on Cemetery Ridge. Geary's Division of the 12th Corps was ordered to the extreme left to occupy Little Round Top. Hancock sent word to General Meade that the position was strong, but that it might be easily turned. He then turned over the command to Slocum, his senior, and returned to Taneytown to report in person. Meade had already ordered a rapid concentration of all his forces at Gettysburg.

For the day, the Confederate commander reported:

"The leading division of Hill met the enemy in advance of Gettysburg on the morning of July 1. Driving back these troops to within a short distance of the town, he there encountered a larger force, with which two of his divisions became engaged. Ewell coming up with two of his divisions by the Heidlersburg road, joined in the engagement. The enemy was driven through Gettysburg with heavy loss, including about 5,000 prisoners and several pieces of artillery. He

retired to a high range of hills south and east of the town. The attack was not pressed that afternoon, the enemy's force being unknown, and it being considered advisable to await the arrival of the rest of our troops. Orders were sent back to hasten their march, and, in the meantime, every effort was made to ascertain the numbers and position of the enemy, and find the most favorable point of attack. It had not been intended to fight a general battle at such a distance from our base, unless attacked by the enemy, but, finding ourselves unexpectedly confronted by the Federal Army, it became a matter of difficulty to withdraw through the mountains with our large trains. . . . Encouraged by the successful issue of the engagement of the first day, and in view of the valuable results that would ensue from the defeat of the army of General Meade, it was thought advisable to renew the attack."

HARVEST

Only the seasons and the years invade
　These quiet wheatfields where the Armies crashed,
And mockingbirds and quail fly unafraid
　Within the forest where the rifles flashed.
Here where the bladed wings of death have mown
　And gleaned their harvestry of golden lives,
The fruitful seeds of corn and wheat are sown,
　And where the cannon smoked, an orchard thrives.

Long are the war years over, with their pain,
　Their passionate tears and fury, and the sun
Lies hot and yellow on the heavy grain,
　And all the fighting on these fields is done.
But in their peace, the quivering heart recalls
　The youth that bled beside these old stone walls.

—AGNES KENDRICK GRAY

By Permission of the Author

GENERAL ROBERT EDWARD LEE

General Robert Edward Lee, third son of the cavalry leader, "Light-Horse Harry" Lee, was born at the family mansion, "Stratford," in Westmoreland County, Va., on January 19, 1807. Entering West Point in 1825 on an appointment secured by Andrew Jackson, he graduated in 1829 with the second honors of his class. In 1837 he was sent west to superintend work on the upper Mississippi. In 1841 he was in charge of the defenses of New York where he remained until the outbreak of the Mexican War. He was wounded at the battle of Chapultepec and brevetted colonel, and took part in the triumphant entry of the army into the City of Mexico on September 14, 1847. In 1852 he was made superintendent of the military academy at West Point. During his administration the discipline was improved and the course of study lengthened. In 1859 he was ordered with a company of Marines to Harper's Ferry to dislodge John Brown. On April 20, 1861, he resigned the colonelcy of the 1st Cavalry and on the 23rd he accepted command of the military forces of Virginia in the Confederate Army. In March, 1862, he was recalled to Richmond to direct the military operations of the Confederacy under President Davis. He succeeded General Johnston in command of the Army of Northern Virginia, which position he held until he surrendered the Army to General Grant at Appomattox, April 9, 1865.

With the end of hostilities General Lee retired to private life, accepting the results of the war with characteristic dignity. He became President of Washington College, now Washington and Lee University, at Lexington, Va. He died at Lexington, October 12, 1870, and was buried beneath the chapel of the University.

"At Gettysburg the future of America was decided forever."—Comte de Paris.

CHAPTER III

FIRST DAY HIGHLIGHTS

Major-General John Fulton Reynolds, killed at Gettysburg while commanding the 1st Corps, was born in Lancaster, Pa., on the 21st day of September, 1820. His father, John Reynolds, also a native of Lancaster County, was the son of William Reynolds, who came to America in 1760 from Ireland. His mother's maiden name was Lydia Moore, daughter of Samuel Moore, who held a commission in the Revolutionary Army. He had an elder brother, William, who served as Admiral in our Navy with great distinction, and also two other brothers who served in the war, one as paymaster, and the other, the youngest of the four, as Quartermaster-General of Pennsylvania.

William and John went first to an excellent school at Lititz, in Lancaster County, going thence to Long Green, Md., and from there they returned to the Lancaster Academy. Through the influence of James Buchanan, they received appointments, one as midshipman in the Navy, and the other as cadet at West Point. John was graduated from West Point on June 22nd, 1841, at the age of twenty-one. He served with distinction during the Mexican War, and at the outbreak of the Civil War entered the Union Army. At the battle of Gaines' Mill, on June 28th, 1862, he was captured, and after a confinement of six weeks in Libby Prison, he was exchanged for General Barksdale.

General Reynolds was six feet tall, with dark hair and eyes. He was erect in carriage and a superb horseman, so much at ease in the saddle as to be able to pick a dime from the ground while riding at full speed. He was killed in the grove now known as Reynolds' Grove on the morn-

ing of July 1st, between 10 and 11 o'clock, while directing the attack of Meredith's Brigade against Archer's Confederate Brigade. His body was first taken to the Seminary, and later to Lancaster, where it was interred in the family graveyard.

. . . .

THE 26TH EMERGENCY REGIMENT

The 26th Emergency Regiment met the advance of Gordon's Brigade of Early's Division of Ewell's Corps in their advance into Gettysburg. Company A consisted of students of the Lutheran Theological Seminary, Pennsylvania (now Gettysburg) College, and citizens of the town. H. M. M. Richards, of Company A, gives the following sketch of the services of the regiment:

"Upon the first indication of an invasion of Pennsylvania, the 26th Regiment, P. V. M., was organized and mustered into the United States service at Harrisburg, under the command of Colonel W. W. Jennings of that city. Company A of this regiment, to which I belonged, was composed of students from the Lutheran Theological Seminary and the Pennsylvania College at Gettysburg, and of citizens of the town; one other company came from Hanover, but a few miles distant.

"On June 23rd we left Harrisburg for Gettysburg, to be used, I believe, as riflemen among the hills at or near Cashtown. A railroad accident prevented this plan from being carried out, and kept us from reaching Gettysburg until the 26th, by which time General Early had reached Cashtown. In accordance with orders received from Major Granville O. Haller, acting aide-de-camp to General Couch, commanding the Department of the Susquehanna, we were marched out on the Chambersburg Pike at 10 A.M., June 26th, for a distance of about three and a half miles, accompanied by Major Robert Bell, who commanded a troop of horse, also raised, I understand, in Gettysburg. Having halted, our colonel, accompanied by

30

Major Bell, rode to the brow of an elevation and there saw General Early's troops a few miles distant.

"We, a few hundred men at most, were in the toils; what should be done? We would gladly have marched to join the Army of the Potomac, under Meade, but where was it? Our colonel, left to his own resources, wisely decided to make an effort to return to Harrisburg, and immediately struck off from the pike, the Confederates capturing many of our rear-guard after a sharp skirmish, and sending their cavalry in pursuit of us. These later overtook us in the afternoon at Witmer's house, about four and a half miles from Gettysburg on the Carlisle Road, where, after an engagement, they were repulsed with some loss. After many vicissitudes, we finally reached Harrisburg, having marched 54 out of 60 consecutive hours, with a loss of some 200 men.

"It should be added that Gettysburg, small town as it was, had already furnished its quota to the army. Moreover, on the first day of the battle, hundreds of the unfortunate men of Reynolds' gallant corps were secreted, sheltered, fed, and aided in every way by the men and women of the town."

• • • •

George W. Sandoe, the first Union soldier killed at THE FIRST
Gettysburg, was a member of Company B Independent SOLDIER
21st Pennsylvania Cavalry. Upon arriving at Gettysburg, KILLED AT
June 26th, 1863, General Gordon sent out a picket line GETTYS-
on the Baltimore Pike. As these pickets reached the BURG
Nathaniel Lightner property, George W. Sandoe and William Lightner, also a member of Company B, approached the pike, coming across the McAllister field from the direction of Rock Creek. Owing to a growth of bushes and trees along the fence, they did not discover the Confederate pickets until they were ordered to halt. Lightner at once jumped his horse across the fence and

31

escaped by riding rapidly down the pike. Sandoe's horse fell in making the leap, and in attempting to escape by riding back in the direction from which he came, Sandoe was shot. He lies buried at Mount Joy Church, in Mount Joy, Adams County.

• • • •

A MYSTER-
IOUS
LETTER

Having passed through Gettysburg on June 26th, General John B. Gordon, of Lee's army, went on to York and Wrightsville before returning on July 1st. In his "Reminiscences of the Gettysburg Campaign" he tells the following story:

"We entered the city of York on Sunday morning. Halting on the main street, where the sidewalks were densely packed, I rode a few rods in advance of my troops, in order to speak to the people from my horse. As I checked him and turned my full dust-begrimed face upon a bevy of ladies very near me, a cry of alarm came from their midst; but after a few words of assurance from me, quiet and apparent confidence were restored. I assured these ladies that the troops behind me, though ill-clad and travel-stained, were good men and brave; that beneath their rough exteriors were hearts as loyal to women as ever beat in the breasts of honorable men; that their own experience and the experience of their mothers, wives, and sisters at home had taught them how painful must be the sight of a hostile army in their town; that under the orders of the Confederate commander-in-chief both private property and non-combatants were safe; that the spirit of vengeance and of rapine had no place in the bosoms of these dust-covered but knightly men; and I closed by pledging to York the head of any soldier under my command who destroyed private property, disturbed the repose of a single home, or insulted a woman.

"As we moved along the street after this episode, a little girl, probably twelve years of age, ran up to my

View overlooking Gettysburg, showing the location of the First Day's Battle. Since 1863 its population has increased from 2,000 to 5,000

The Reynolds' Statue is in the position where the General's death occurred, and shows his attitude shortly before. General Buford's statue is at the right center, and the first gun fired by the Union forces may be seen just below it.

The Pennsylvania Monument,
with bronze figures of distinguished officers and a roster of
all Pennsylvanians in battle

The Gettysburg Seminary
(Lutheran Theological Seminary in 1863), used as an observation point and hospital

Barlow's Knoll. The extreme right of the Union line
on the First Day

horse and handed me a large bouquet of flowers in the center of which was a note in delicate handwriting, purporting to give the numbers and describe the position of the Union forces of Wrightsville, toward which I was advancing. I carefully read and reread this strange note. It bore no signature and contained no assurance of sympathy for the Southern cause, but it was so terse and explicit in its terms as to compel my confidence. The second day we were in front of Wrightsville, and from the high ridge on which this note suggested that I halt and examine the position of the Union troops, I eagerly scanned the prospect with my field-glasses, in order to verify the truth of the mysterious communication or detect its misrepresentations.

"There, in full view of us, was the town, just as described, nestling on the banks of the Susquehanna. There was the blue line of soldiers guarding the approach, drawn up, as indicated, along an intervening ridge and across the pike. There was the long bridge spanning the Susquehanna and connecting the town with Columbia on the other bank. Most important of all, there was the deep gorge or ravine running off to the right and extending around the left bank of the Federal line and to the river below the bridge. Not an inaccurate detail in that note could be discovered. I did not hesitate, therefore, to adopt its suggestion of moving down the gorge in order to throw my command on the flank, or possibly in the rear of the Union troops, and force them to a rapid retreat or surrender. The result of this movement vindicated the strategic wisdom of my unknown and—judging by the handwriting—woman correspondent, whose note was none the less martial because embedded in roses, and whose evident genius for war, had occasion offered, might have made her a captain equal to Catherine."

THE FLAG OF THE 16TH MAINE

A marker showing the position of the 16th Maine Infantry Regiment on the afternoon of the first day's battle stands at the intersection of Doubleday Avenue and the Mummasburg Road, and contains the following inscription:

POSITION HELD JULY 1, 1863, AT 4 O'CLOCK P.M.
BY THE 16TH MAINE INFANTRY
1ST BRIG., 2ND DIV., 1ST CORPS
WHILE THE REST OF THE DIVISION WAS RETIRING, THE
REGIMENT HAVING MOVED FROM THE POSITION AT THE
LEFT WHERE ITS MONUMENT STANDS, UNDER ORDERS
TO HOLD THIS POSITION AT ANY COST.
IT LOST ON THIS FIELD
KILLED 11, WOUNDED 62, CAPTURED 159
OUT OF 275 ENGAGED

When almost surrounded, the regiment withdrew to the left of the railroad cut to help cover the withdrawal of Stewart's battery, which was also almost surrounded. The regiment had two flags, the Stars and Stripes and the flag of Maine.

Finally, assaulted by the flank and rear, they determined not to surrender their colors, but tore them from their staffs and into small bits, each man taking a star or a bit of silk which he placed in his pocket. Some of these fragments were carried through the southern prisons and finally home to Maine, where they are still treasured as precious relics by the relatives and friends of the brave men of the regiment.

• • • •

THE BARLOW-GORDON INCIDENT

Barlow's Knoll, a short distance northeast of Gettysburg, is named in honor of Brigadier-General Francis C. Barlow, in command of the 1st Division of the 11th Corps. In his "Reminiscences of the Civil War," General Gordon describes his meeting with Barlow:

"Returning from the banks of the Susquehanna, and meeting at Gettysburg, July 1, 1863, the advance of Lee's

34

forces, my command was thrown quickly and squarely on the right flank of the Union Army. A more timely arrival never occurred. The battle had been raging for four or five hours. The Confederate General Archer, with a large part of his brigade, had been captured. Heth and Scales, Confederate generals, had been wounded. The ranking Union officer on the field, General Reynolds, had been killed, and General Hancock was assigned to command. The battle, upon the issue of which hung, perhaps, the fate of the Confederacy, was in full blast. The Union forces, at first driven back, now reënforced, were again advancing and pressing back Lee's left and threatening to envelop it. The Confederates were stubbornly contesting every foot of ground, but the Southern left was slowly yielding. A few moments more and the day's battle might have been ended by a complete turning of Lee's flank. I was ordered to move at once to the aid of the heavily pressed Confederates. With a ringing yell, my command rushed upon the line posted to protect the Union right. Here occurred a hand-to-hand struggle. That protecting Union line, once broken, left my command not only on the right flank, but obliquely in rear of it.

"Any troops that were ever marshalled would, under like conditions, have been as surely and swiftly shattered. Under the concentrated fire from front and flank, the marvel is that they escaped. In the midst of the wild disorder in his ranks, and through a storm of bullets, a Union officer was seeking to rally his men for a final stand. He, too, went down pierced by a minie ball. Riding forward with my rapidly advancing lines, I discovered that brave officer lying upon his back, with the July sun pouring its rays into his pale face. He was surrounded by the Union dead, and his own life seemed to be rapidly ebbing out. Quickly I dismounted and lifted his head. I gave him water from my canteen, and asked his name and the

character of his wounds. He was Major-General Francis C. Barlow, of New York, and of Howard's Corps. The ball had entered his body in front and passed out near the spinal cord, paralyzing him in legs and arms. Neither of us had the remotest thought that he could survive many hours. I summoned several soldiers who were looking after the wounded, and directed them to place him upon a litter and carry him to the shade in the rear. Before parting, he asked me to take from his pocket a package of letters and destroy them. They were from his wife. He had one request to make of me. That request was that, if I lived to the end of the war and ever met Mrs. Barlow, I would tell her of our meeting on the field of Gettysburg and his thoughts of her in his last moments. He wished to assure me that he died doing his duty at the front, that he was willing to give his life for his country, and that his deepest regret was that he must die without looking upon her face again. I learned that Mrs. Barlow was with the Union Army, and near the battlefield. When it is remembered how closely Mrs. Gordon followed me, it will not be difficult to realize that my sympathies were especially stirred by the announcement that his wife was so near to him. Passing through the day's battle unhurt, I despatched, at its close, under a flag of truce, the promised message to Mrs. Barlow. I assured her that she should have safe escort to her husband's side.

"In the desperate encounters of the two succeeding days, and the retreat of Lee's army, I thought no more of Barlow, except to number him with the noble dead of the two armies who have so gloriously met their fate. The ball, however, had struck no vital point, and Barlow slowly recovered, though his fate was unknown to me. The following summer, in battles near Richmond, my kinsman with the same initials, General J. B. Gordon of North Carolina, was killed. Barlow, who had recovered,

saw the announcement of his death, and entertained no doubt that he was the Gordon whom he had met on the field of Gettysburg. To me, therefore, Barlow was dead; to Barlow I was dead. Nearly fifteen years passed before either of us was undeceived. During my second term in the United States Senate, the Hon. Clarkson Potter of New York was the member of the House of Representatives. He invited me to dinner in Washington to meet a General Barlow who had served in the Union Army. Potter knew nothing of the Gettysburg incident. I had heard that there was another Barlow in the Union Army, and supposed of course, that it was this Barlow with whom I was to dine. Barlow had a similar reflection as to the Gordon he was to meet. Seated at Clarkson Potter's table, I asked Barlow: 'General, are you related to the Barlow who was killed at Gettysburg?' He replied: 'Why, I am the man, sir. Are you related to the Gordon who killed me?' 'I am the man, sir,' I responded. No words of mine can convey any conception of the emotions awakened by these startling announcements. Nothing short of an actual resurrection of the dead could have amazed either of us more. Thenceforward, until his untimely death in 1896, the friendship between us which was born amidst the thunders of Gettysburg was cherished by both."

• • • •

General Gordon gives an account of an amusing incident of the first day:

"Late in the afternoon of this first day's battle, when the firing had greatly decreased along most of the lines, General Ewell and I were riding through the streets of Gettysburg. In a previous battle he had lost one of his legs, but prided himself on the efficiency of the wooden one which he used in its place. As we rode together, a body of Union soldiers, posted behind some dwellings and

GENERAL
EWELL IS
HIT BY A
BULLET

fences on the outskirts of the town, suddenly opened a brisk fire. A number of Confederates were killed or wounded, and I heard the ominous thud of a minie ball as it struck General Ewell at my side. I quickly asked: 'Are you hurt, sir?' 'No, no,' he replied; 'I'm not hurt. But suppose that ball had struck you: we would have had the trouble of carrying you off the field, sir. You see how much better fixed I am for a fight than you are. It don't hurt a bit to be shot in a wooden leg.'

"Ewell was a most interesting and eccentric character. It is said that in his early manhood he had been disappointed in a love affair, and had never fully recovered from its effects. The fair maiden to whom he had given his affections had married another man; but Ewell, like the truest of knights, carried her image in his heart through long years. When he was promoted to the rank of brigadier or major-general, he evidenced the constancy of his affections by placing upon his staff the son of the woman whom he had loved in his youth. The meddlesome Fates, who seem to revel in the romances of lovers, had decreed that Ewell should be shot in battle and become the object of solicitude and tender nursing by this lady, Mrs. Brown, who had been for many years a widow. Her gentle ministrations soothed his weary weeks of suffering, a marriage ensued, and with it came the realization of Ewell's long-deferred hope. He was a most devoted husband. He never seemed to realize, however, that marriage had changed her name, for he proudly presented her to his friends as 'My wife, Mrs. Brown, sir.' "

• • • •

THE
SCHOOL-
TEACHERS'
REGIMENT

The 151st Pennsylvania Infantry, commanded by Lieutenant-Colonel George F. McFarland, included Company D, made up mainly of the instructors and students of the Lost Creek Academy, of McAlisterville, Juniata County, of which Colonel McFarland was principal. For

38

this reason it was called the "School-teachers' Regiment." The material throughout was excellent, many of the men being experienced marksmen. The regiment went into battle with 21 officers and 446 men, and sustained a loss in killed, wounded, and missing of 337, or over 75 per cent.

The casualties of the 26th North Carolina Regiment, against which they were engaged, were 588 out of 800, just about the same percentage.

Colonel McFarland lost his right leg and had the left permanently disabled, but survived until 1891. On the twenty-fifth anniversary of the battle, he delivered the dedicatory address at the unveiling of the regimental monument, exactly twenty-five years to the hour after his engagement in battle.

. . . .

An incident, similar to that described by Browning in his poem "An Incident of the French Camp," occurred at the railroad cut early on the first day. AN INCI-DENT OF THE FIRST DAY

An officer of the 6th Wisconsin Regiment, active in the capture of the Mississippians belonging to the 2nd and 42nd Regiments, who had taken shelter in the railroad cut after turning the right of Cutler's line, approached Colonel Rufus R. Dawes after the engagement was over. Colonel Dawes supposed, from the erect appearance of the man, that he had come for further orders, but his compressed lips told a different story. With great effort the officer said: "Tell them at home I died like a man and a soldier." He then opened his coat, showed a ghastly wound on his breast, and dropped dead.

"The Battle of Gettysburg settled the question whether or not the Government would be of the people, by the people, and for the people."—ANDREW D. WHITE.

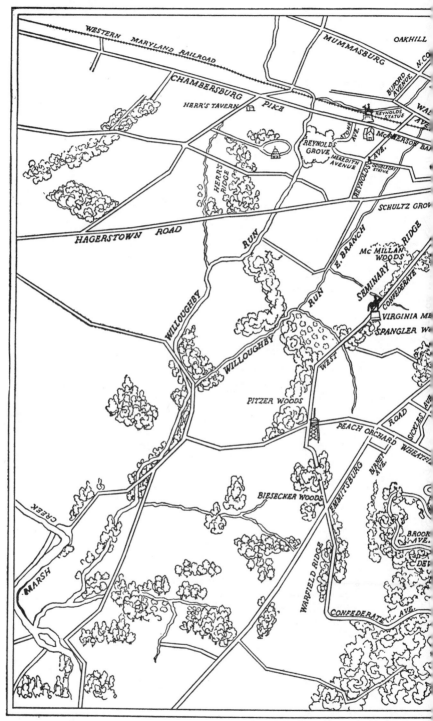

Locations, Buildings and Avenues

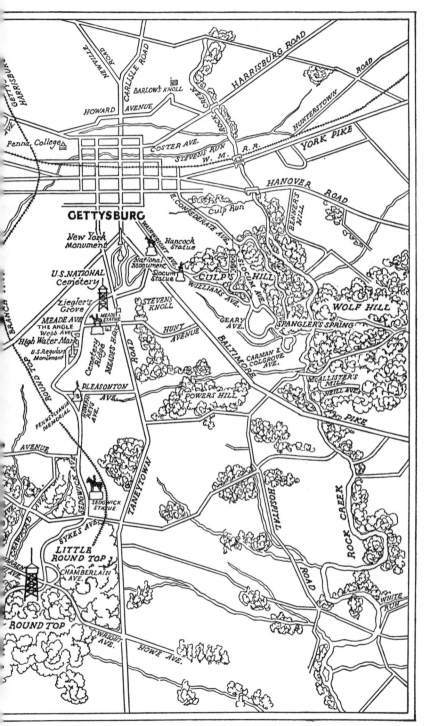

as referred to in this book

DAYS OF DREAD

(Following are the impressions of Mrs. Robert Horner, recorded some years after the battle. She was the wife of Dr. Robert Horner, who lived opposite the College Church, in a house which had been the home of Thaddeus Stevens during his residence in Gettysburg. To this house friends in the Cumberland Valley sent the first supplies of food for the almost starving multitudes. Mrs. Horner was one of many Gettysburg women who cared for the wounded and dying. Indeed, the woman who did not devote herself to nursing was the rare exception.)

Soon after the battle began, General Reynolds ordered all the houses on the west side of the town vacated. Hurriedly, I gathered my children together and accepted the invitation of Dr. Baugher to go to his house on the College campus. This was leaving the frying-pan for the fire; shells were falling so thick and fast that we soon set out for home. Alas, our Union artillery was being driven down Seminary Hill, and the street on which we lived was full of soldiers. Passing up an alley to our public square, where a number of bands were playing, we stood watching the coming in of Archer's troops as prisoners. Mrs. Carson, wife of the cashier of the bank, asked us into her house. We stood for some time at one of the windows watching the battle, and had just withdrawn, when a shell came in the window and blew out in the room. Had it exploded, some of us would certainly have been killed. We were thankful that all rebel shells were not perfect in construction. That same morning we found bullets in the room where the baby was sleeping.

Presently word was sent to the citizens to go to their cellars, as the enemy were driving our men and the fighting would be from house to house on our streets. Mrs. Carson proposed that we should go to the small vault of the

bank, which we did, nineteen women, and children, two dogs and a cat.

About the middle of the afternoon of the second day (Thursday), when the firing had ceased, I asked a Confederate officer if I could get to my home, and when he said I could I started, but what sights met my eyes as I stepped out into the street: A dead horse just before the door; a soldier breaking open a cellar-door with an ax; in the streets the direst collection of groceries of all kinds; boxes and barrels, wagons and guns; dead men and blood everywhere; and wounded men being carried here and there wherever an open doorway offered rest and security.

Some of the citizens left their houses and went into the country, but the greater number stayed and spent their time in their cellars. Those who left their homes found them sadly out of order on their return, ransacked in search of valuables. Once I went past a number of Confederate soldiers with a bottle of chloroform wrapped in my apron. I was relieved to get through without being questioned. In many cases carpets were saturated with blood and unfit for further use; walls were bloodstained, as well as books that were used for pillows.

When the battle was over our houses were filled with the wounded; provisions were well-nigh exhausted; and 35,000 soldiers were left to be cared for and fed. The country people who had suffered in many ways were unable to bring in any supplies. The July heat was intense, and there were swarms of flies that were attracted by the horrible stench from the immense quantity of dead and decaying matter and filth of every kind. During the day we did not suffer as much as at night, when we were obliged to close the windows and doors to avoid exposure to the outside air. Truly those were days when we lived "mid scenes of confusion and creature complaints" with human suffering and death grown, alas! too familiar to all.

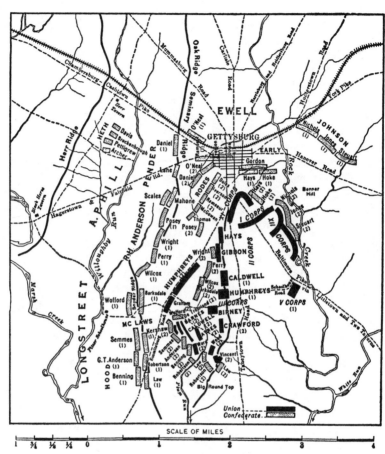

SCALE OF MILES

Positions of the Second Day's Battle

CHAPTER IV

THE SECOND DAY'S BATTLE

ON the second and third days the battle shifted to the country south and southeast of Gettysburg. General Meade arrived on the field from Taneytown, Md., at 1 A.M., July 2nd, and at once established his headquarters at the Leister House, on the Taneytown Road, in rear of the line of the 2nd Corps. As soon as it was light he inspected the position already occupied and made arrangements for posting the several corps as soon as they should reach the ground.

Starting on the right with Slocum's 12th Corps, Williams' Division extended from Rock Creek by way of Spangler's Spring to Culp's Hill, with Geary's Division on the hill. The line between Culp's Hill and Cemetery Hill was held by Wadsworth's Division of the 1st Corps. Barlow's Division of the 11th Corps under Ames was located at the foot of East Cemetery Hill. Carman, Colgrove, Slocum, Geary, and Wainwright avenues follow these lines of battle. THE UNION LINE OF BATTLE

On Cemetery Hill, across the Baltimore Pike, the line was held by Schurz and on his left Steinwehr, both of the 11th Corps. Robinson's Division of the 1st Corps extended across the

Taneytown Road to Ziegler's Grove. Beyond lay Hancock's 2nd Corps, with the Divisions of Hays, Gibbon, and Caldwell from right to left. To the left of Hancock, Sickles' 3rd Corps, consisting of the Divisions of Humphreys and Birney, prolonged the line to the vicinity of Little Round Top. Beginning at the Taneytown Road, Hancock and Sedgwick avenues follow these lines of battle.

Arriving later in the day, the 5th Corps, under General Sykes, was posted on the Baltimore Pike, at the Rock Creek crossing. Later it occupied the ground about Round Top to the left of the 3rd Corps. The 6th Corps, under General Sedgwick, reaching the field still later after a march of over 30 miles, was posted in reserve back of Round Top, from which position portions were moved as circumstances demanded. The lines held by the 5th and 6th Corps coincide with Sykes, Ayres, Wright, and Howe avenues.

Gamble's and Devin's brigades of Buford's Cavalry, which had had an active part in the battle of the first day, were on the left between Cemetery and Seminary Ridges until 10 A.M. when they were ordered, by some mistake, to move to Westminster, Md., before the arrival of Gregg's Division on its way from Hanover, and Merritt's brigade of Buford's Division from Mechanicsburg (now Thurmont), Md.

General Meade's line, shaped like a fishhook, was about 3 miles long. The right faced east, the center over Cemetery Hill, north, and the left from Cemetery Hill to Round Top nearly west. The whole line was supported by artillery brigades belonging to the different corps.

General Lee's line was nearly the same shape as General Meade's but, being the outer line, was about 6 miles long. On the right, facing the two Round Tops, were Hood's and McLaws' Divisions of Longstreet's Corps. On the left of McLaws, extending along the line of Seminary Ridge, were the divisions of Anderson and Pender of Hill's Corps, with Heth's Division in the rear in reserve. On the left of Pender, extending through the town along the line of West Middle Street, was Rodes' Division of Ewell's Corps, then Early's and Johnson's Divisions, the latter reaching to Benner's Hill, east of Rock Creek. Pickett's Division of Longstreet's Corps was at Chambersburg, guarding trains, and Law's Brigade of Hood's Division of Longstreet's Corps at New Guilford, guarding the rear. The latter arrived at noon on the 2nd in time to participate in the day's engagement. Pickett's Division arrived later and was not engaged until the afternoon of the 3rd. The artillery was posted according to the different corps to which it was attached.

General Lee's line coincides with the present

47

West Confederate Avenue along Seminary and Warfield or Snyder Ridges, west of the town, then runs through the town to coincide with East Confederate Avenue. The distance between the Union and Confederate lines is three-fourths of a mile to a mile.

Military critics agree that General Meade held the stronger position. Both flanks presented precipitous and rocky fronts, difficult to attack, and it was possible to send reinforcements by short distances from point to point.

SICKLES' CHANGE OF LINE

As already stated, General Sickles' 3rd Corps was on the left of General Hancock's 2nd Corps on Cemetery Ridge, and Birney's Division was near the base of Little Round Top, replacing Geary's Division after its withdrawal to be posted on Culp's Hill. Humphreys' Division was on low ground to the right between Cemetery Ridge and the Emmitsburg Road.

Anxious to know what was in his front, Sickles sent the Berdan Sharpshooters and the 3rd Maine Infantry forward on a reconnaissance. On reaching the Pitzer Woods, beyond the Emmitsburg Road, they found the Confederates there in force, and after a sharp engagement with Wilcox's Brigade, withdrew and reported.

Believing that Lee planned a flank movement on his line, and that the Emmitsburg Road afforded better positions for the artillery, Sickles moved his Corps forward and posted Humphreys'

Stevens' Knoll. Arriving on Stevens' Knoll at the end of the First Day, General Slocum brought supporting troops. The lunettes protecting the cannon remain intact

Dormitory of Gettysburg College. The dormitory of Gettysburg (then Pennsylvania) College sheltered many Union and Confederate wounded

Wheatfield. Scene of carnage on the Second Day. (See page 52)

Guns Supporting Pickett's Charge. These guns, from Seminary Ridge, took part in the great artillery duel which preceded Pickett's Charge

Division on the right along the Emmitsburg Road and his left extending to the Peach Orchard. Birney's Division prolonged the line from the Peach Orchard across the Wheatfield to Devil's Den. This new line formed a salient at the Peach Orchard and therefore presented two fronts, one to the west, the other to the south.

About 3 P.M. Sickles was called to General Meade's headquarters to a conference of corps commanders. Upon the sound of artillery, the conference adjourned, and Meade, Sickles, and Warren, Meade's Chief Engineer, rode to inspect Sickles' change of line. The artillery was already engaged, and believing it too late to make any changes since the enemy was present, Meade decided to attempt to hold the new position by sending in supports. After reviewing the new line, General Warren left the other members of the party and rode up Little Round Top. He found the height unoccupied except by the personnel of a signal station.

Lee as well as Meade occupied the forenoon GENERAL in the arrangement of his line of battle. After a LEE'S PLAN conference with Ewell, he decided to attack Meade's left. In his report, Lee says:

> "It was determined to make the principal attack upon the enemy's left, and endeavor to gain a position from which it was thought that our artillery could be brought to bear with effect. Longstreet was directed to place the division of McLaws and Hood on the right

of Hill, partially enveloping the enemy's left, which he was to drive in.

"General Hill was ordered to threaten the enemy's center to prevent reinforcements being drawn to either wing, and coöperate with his right division in Longstreet's attack.

"General Ewell was instructed to make a simultaneous demonstration upon the enemy's right, to be converted into a real attack should opportunity offer."

When General Lee arranged this plan of attack he believed Meade's left terminated at the Peach Orchard; he did not know that Sickles' advance line extended to the left from the salient at the Peach Orchard to Devil's Den. In plain view of the Union signal station on Little Round Top, some of his forces were compelled to make a wide detour via the Black Horse Tavern on the Fairfield Road in order to avoid observation.

LITTLE
ROUND TOP

Meanwhile, General Warren on Little Round Top saw the importance of the hill as a tactical position on Meade's left. The signal officers were preparing to leave; he ordered them to remain and to keep waving their flags so as to lead the Confederates to believe that the hill was occupied. He dispatched a messenger to Devil's Den, where a Union battery was posted, with an order that a shot be fired to produce confusion in the woods in front, through which Hood's forces were supposed to be advancing. Seeing the reflection of the sunlight from Confederate muskets, he realized that if this important posi-

tion were to be held, it would be necessary to get troops there without delay.

Quickly he sent a member of his staff to Sickles for troops. Sickles said none could be spared. Warren sent another staff officer to Meade, who immediately ordered Sykes to move his Corps to Little Round Top. Barnes' Division of this Corps had already been called for by Sickles to defend his line, and three brigades, Vincent's, Tilton's, and Sweitzer's, were moving toward the Wheatfield. Learning of the need of troops on Little Round Top, Vincent moved back, skirted the east side of Little Round Top, and went into position between Little and Big Round Top, arriving just before the Confederates from Hood's right advanced over Big Round Top.

Having watched these movements, Warren rode down to the crossing of what is now Sykes Avenue and the Wheatfield Road. There he met Colonel O'Rorke, in command of the 140th New York, and ordered his regiments, together with Hazlett's battery, to the crest of the hill. With the addition of Weed's Brigade, the combined forces held the Round Tops. There was a desperate engagement in which both Unionists and Confederates displayed courage of a very high order. The Union soldiers were victorious, and Meade's left was henceforth secure against further attack.

After the struggle for the possession of Little Round Top, the other Confederate brigades of Hood and McLaws advanced rapidly. A lack of coördination in their movement allowed Meade to bring up supports. Three brigades of Anderson's Division of Hill's Corps advanced against Humphreys' line, in the following order: Wilcox, Perry, Wright. Wounded, General Pender was unable to direct Posey and Mahone in support of Wright, and Wright was obliged to withdraw. Humphreys was compelled to change front in order to meet the assault on his flanks. This maneuver served to stay the Confederate attack for a brief time. The Valley of Death between the Round Tops and the opposite height was now a seething mass of opposing forces, enshrouded in clouds of smoke.

Meade had already depleted his right to support his left by withdrawing all of Slocum's 12th Corps except Greene's Brigade. He now sent all of the 5th Corps to the left and ordered Caldwell's Division from the left of Hancock's 2nd Corps south of the Angle to the Wheatfield. Willard's Brigade on Hays' line of the 2nd Corps was ordered to advance and oppose the Confederate, Barksdale, who, after crossing the Emmitsburg Road north of the Peach Orchard and the field beyond, reached Watson's Union battery posted on the Trostle farm. General Sickles was severely and Barksdale mortally wounded.

Wofford's Brigade of McLaws' Division broke through the salient at the Peach Orchard and reached the valley between Devil's Den and Little Round Top, where they were met by a charge of the Pennsylvania Reserves of Crawford's Division, led by McCandless, some of whose men fought in sight of their own homes. Wofford was obliged to withdraw to and beyond the Wheatfield; the Reserves advanced across the valley from their position on the north of Little Round Top and reached the stone wall on the east side of the Wheatfield. Here they remained until after Pickett's charge on the 3rd, when they advanced against the Confederates who had succeeded in regaining control of that part of the field.

About the time when Sickles was wounded, Meade directed Hancock to assume command of Sickles' Corps in addition to his own. Meade in person led Lockwood's Brigade, brought from the extreme right, against the Confederate advance. Newton, now in command of the 1st Corps, sent in Doubleday's Division. With these troops Hancock checked the advance of the Confederate brigades of Barksdale, Wilcox, Perry, and Wright, while Sykes checked the advance of Hood and McLaws. Brigades of the 6th Corps reached the field toward the close of the engagement. Withdrawing from the Wheatfield Road, Bigelow's battery made a determined

stand at the Trostle buildings and succeeded in checking the Confederate advance until the gap on Sickles' first line was protected by a line of guns. Most of the Confederate brigades got no farther than Plum Run, except Wright's, which actually reached the line of guns on Hancock's front before it was obliged to withdraw. During the repulse of the Confederate advance, the 1st Minnesota regiment of Harrow's Brigade of Gibbon's Division of Hancock's Corps was ordered by Hancock to oppose Wilcox's and Perry's brigades, rapidly advancing against Hancock's left. The Minnesota regiment moved up at once and succeeded in repelling the attack, but only after losing eighty-two per cent of its men.

Though seriously threatened, Meade's line held, and after the repulse of Wright, the attack ended. During the night the line was prolonged to the top of Big Round Top. The Confederates remained west of Plum Run, except at Big Round Top, where they intrenched along the western slope.

EWELL'S ATTACK ON MEADE'S RIGHT

Ordered by Lee to begin his attack on Meade's right as a means of drawing troops away from the main attack on Meade's left, General Ewell had failed to hear the artillery, whose sound did not carry. At 4 o'clock instead of 3, Confederate batteries from Benner's Hill opened upon Culp's Hill, East Cemetery Hill, and West Cemetery Hill, on which the Union forces were stationed.

The Union troops had had time thoroughly to protect themselves by breastworks and fortifications, but they were greatly depleted by the removal of troops to Meade's left. At sundown the Confederate batteries ceased to fire and the infantry advanced, General Johnson against Culp's Hill, General Early against East Cemetery Hill. Rodes, who was directed to move against West Cemetery Hill, was unable to obey instructions. General Walker, who had been sent east to Brinkerhoff Ridge in the forenoon, to guard Ewell's flank, and who was expected to assist in this attack, was prevented by meeting part of the Union cavalry of Gregg's Division that had arrived via Hanover on the forenoon of the 2nd. After an engagement with Gregg, Walker moved up to assist Johnson, but too late to be of service, as the attack on Culp's Hill had ended.

The attack was conducted with the greatest dash and daring, in part up rough slopes of woodland over heaped boulders. On East Cemetery Hill the fight among the Union guns was hand to hand, and clubbed muskets, stones, and rammers were used to drive back the assailants. After sunset a bright moon illuminated the field. The Union troops stood firm, and at 10 o'clock the Confederates desisted, having captured only a few Union entrenchments. These they held until early the following morning.

Lee's assaults on Meade's left had failed to accomplish anything decisive. While Sickles' advance-line was driven back and most of the field, including the Peach Orchard, the Wheatfield, Devil's Den, and the base of Big Round Top, was occupied by the Confederates, Meade's line was practically intact from the crest of Big Round Top on the left to near Spangler's Spring on the right. On the slopes of Round Top, on Cemetery Hill and Culp's Hill, the advantage of the defensive positions multiplied the forces of the defenders in comparison with the attackers at least three to one. Prodigies of valor were performed by both armies, and courage of the highest order was displayed in attack and in the defense. Casualties were very heavy on both sides. General Meade estimated that his losses were sixty-five per cent of the total losses for the three days. At the end of the day he made the following report:

"July 2, 1863, 8 P.M. The enemy attacked me about 4 P.M. this day, and, after one of the severest contests of the war, was repulsed at all points. We have suffered considerably in killed and wounded. Among the former are Brigadier Generals Paul and Zook, and among the wounded are Generals Sickles, Barlow, Graham, and Warren slightly. We have taken a large number of prisoners. I shall remain in my present position to-morrow, but am not prepared to say, until better advised of the condition of the army, whether my operations will be of an offensive or defensive character."

Later in the night, at a council of war held by Meade with his corps commanders—Gibbon, Williams, Sykes, Newton, Howard, Hancock, Sedgwick, and Slocum—sentiment favored remaining and fighting a defensive battle. As Lee attacked both wings of Meade's line on the 2nd it was expected that if another attack were made it would be on the center. This expectation was correct—Wright's attack on the 2nd, when he succeeded in reaching Meade's line south of the Angle, led Lee to believe that this was the most vulnerable point.

General Lee had more definite plans:

> "The result of this day's operations induced the belief that, with proper concert of action, and with the increased support that the positions gained on the right would enable the artillery to render the assaulting column, we should ultimately succeed, and it was accordingly determined to continue the attack."

The general plan was unchanged. Longstreet, re-enforced by Pickett's three brigades, which arrived near the battlefield during the afternoon of the 2nd, was ordered to attack the next morning, and General Ewell was directed to assail the enemy's right at the same time. The latter, during the night, re-enforced General Johnson with three brigades from Rodes' and Early's Divisions.

STRENGTH COMPARISON

The strength of Meade's army was as follows:

PRESENT FOR DUTY, EQUIPPED, JUNE 30, 1863

ARMY OF THE POTOMAC	Head-qts.	Infantry	Cavalry	Artillery	Aggre-gate
General Headquarters....	50				50
Provost-Guard	1,529				1,529
Engineers' Brigade......	946				946
Guards and Orderlies....	49				49
Signal Corps	6				6
1st Army Corps		9,403		619	10,022
2nd Army Corps........		12,363	82	551	12,996
3rd Army Corps........		11,247		677	11,924
5th Army Corps		11,954		555	12,509
6th Army Corps		14,516	124	1,039	15,679
11th Army Corps		9,197	52	644	9,893
12th Army Corps		8,193		396	8,589
Cavalry Corps			13,670	854	14,524
Artillery Reserve		335		2,211	2,546
Totals............	2,580	77,208	13,928	7,546	101,262

Allowing for detachments for train-guards and other services, the actual number present and engaged was about 84,000.

The Army of Northern Virginia, according to the only obtainable record, numbered 6,116 officers, and 68,343 men, a total of 74,459.

General Longstreet estimates Lee's strength at Gettysburg as 75,568. Colonel Walter H. Taylor, Lee's Adjutant-General, puts the figures at 67,000. The Comte de Paris estimates Meade's effective forces as 82,000 to 84,000, and Lee's 68,000 to 69,000.

CHAPTER V

INCIDENTS OF THE
SECOND DAY

THE Roger House is located on the west side of the Emmitsburg Road, about a mile south of Gettysburg, midway between Meade's line of battle on Cemetery Ridge and Lee's line on Seminary Ridge. On the afternoon of July 2nd, after Sickles advanced his corps from its first position to the Emmitsburg Road, it was surrounded by the right of the new line. The 1st Massachusetts Regiment, whose monument stands adjacent to the house, held this part of the line, and was hotly engaged when the brigades of Wilcox and Wright advanced during the assault of Longstreet on the Union left on the afternoon of the 2nd. During Pickett's Charge, on the afternoon of the 3rd, the house was again surrounded by fighting men.

While the battle raged on all sides, a granddaughter of the owner, Miss Josephine Miller, remained, and, notwithstanding the great danger, baked bread and biscuits for the hungry soldiers. In 1896, Miss Miller, then Mrs. Slyder, paid a visit to her old home, and related the interesting story of her experience to Mr. Wilfred Pearse, of Boston, Mass., a visitor to Gettysburg at the same time. After his return he published the following article.

"The veterans of the 1st Massachusetts Infantry Regiment will be glad to learn that the only woman member of the 3rd Army Corps 'Veterans' Association,' Mrs. Slyder, née Miss Josephine Miller, granddaughter of farmer Roger, owner of the farm near which the 1st Massachusetts monument stands, is visiting her old home on the battleground where she stood from sunrise to sunset for two days of the battle making hot biscuits for the Boys in Blue. She refused to take money for the bread, and

refused to stop her work even when Confederate shells were bursting around the house. She told me the other day that when her stock of flour was almost exhausted six members of the 1st Massachusetts kindly volunteered to go out and steal three sacks of flour from General Sickles' commissary stores. In an hour's time they returned with flour, raisins, currants, and a whole sheep, with which a rattling good meal was made.

"The old range still stands in the kitchen, and in it, at the last reunion of the 3rd Corps, Mrs. Slyder cooked a dinner for General Sickles."

. . . .

SPANGLER'S
SPRING

This spring, which takes its name from Abraham Spangler, its owner at the time of the battle, is located at the southeast corner of Culp's Hill. Inasmuch as it was used by soldiers of both armies during the battle, and since then by thousands of tourists, it is an interesting feature of the field. Only during the drought of 1930 has it failed to give forth a copious flow of cool, pure water. At the time of the battle it was surrounded by a wall of flat stones with a flagstone cover over the top. These were removed and a canopy top erected.

The 12th Corps of the Army of the Potomac occupied this part of Meade's line on the night of the first day and until the afternoon of the 2nd, when the troops were ordered to the left to help repel Longstreet's assault. Until this time the spring was used only by the Union troops. During their absence, the Confederates under Johnson moved up and took possession of part of the vacated line. In the early morning of the third day, the Union forces, who had returned from the left during the night of the 2nd, attacked Johnson, drove him out and succeeded in regaining possession of the line that had been vacated by them on the afternoon of the 2nd, including the spring.

The story that a truce was entered into between the opposing forces on the night of the 2nd and that they met in large numbers at the spring to get water is a mistake. The captured and wounded of the Union forces were allowed access to it along with the Confederates who were there at the time, but there was no truce. When armies were encamped, pickets from the opposing lines would sometimes get together, usually to trade coffee and tobacco, but this was never done when a battle was in progress.

The following extract from the address of Captain Joseph Matchett at the dedication of the monument erected by the 46th Pennsylvania Infantry Regiment, shows that there was no truce:

"Some time in the night (2nd), we were ordered to return to our works on Culp's Hill. It seems Captain Selfridge of Company H had taken some of his men's canteens and gone ahead to Spangler's Spring to fill them, when he discovered 'Johnnies' also filling their canteens. He backed out with the best grace he could command, and reported it to the colonel. Colonel McDougall, the brigade commander, did not believe it and got very angry, but the colonel of the regiment insisted on deploying his men, and sent a skirmish line, who found the enemy as stated and saved many lives."

. . . .

Among those who faced death in the desperate charge on the Union right on East Cemetery Hill, July 2nd, Colonel I. E. Avery, of North Carolina, in command of Hoke's Brigade, bore a gallant part. At the head of the column he led his men up the slope of Cemetery Hill and, a conspicuous mark, fell mortally wounded. COLONEL AVERY'S LOST GRAVE

Unable to speak, he drew a card from his pocket and wrote the following: "Tell father that I died with my face toward the enemy." In the retreat from Gettysburg, his body was taken along to be delivered to his family,

but when the army reached Williamsport the Potomac was too high to cross. There, in the cemetery overlooking the river, the remains were interred in an oak coffin under a pine tree. He was buried in his uniform by the men who saw him fall. Thirty years after, Judge A. C. Avery, of the Supreme Court of North Carolina, a resident of Morgantown, and Captain J. A. McPherson of Fayette, N. C., both veterans of the Confederacy, came to Williamsport with the object of locating Colonel Avery's grave. Their search was fruitless. . . . .

THE
LEISTER
HOUSE

On his arrival, General Meade established his headquarters at the Leister House, one of the oldest houses in the community, located at the intersection of Meade Avenue and the Taneytown Road. At the time of the battle it was the property of a widow, Mrs. Leister. It now belongs to the Government, and a bronze plate marks it as Meade's Headquarters. It is built of logs, chinked and weatherboarded with rough pine boards, pierced by bullet-holes and scarred by shells.

Inside there are two rooms, a small kitchen at the west, and a larger room at the east. In the latter, Meade held a council of war after the battle of the 2nd had ended, summoning his Corps commanders between 9 and 10 o'clock to consult them as to what action, if any, should be taken on the 3rd. Generals Sedgwick, Slocum, Hancock, Howard, Sykes, Newton, Birney, Williams, and Gibbon were present. The following questions were asked:

(1) Under existing circumstances is it advisable for this army to remain in its present position, or to retire to another nearer its base of supplies?

(2) It being determined to remain in present position, shall the army attack or wait the attack of the enemy?

(3) If we wait attack, how long?

The replies were:

Gibbon: (1) Correct position of the army, but would not retreat. (2) In no condition to attack, in his opinion. (3) Until he moves.

Williams: (1) Stay. (2) Wait attack. (3) One day.

Birney and Sykes: Same as General Williams.

Newton: (1) Correct position of the army, but would not retreat. (2) By all means not attack. (3) If we wait it will give them a chance to cut our line.

Howard: (1) Remain. (2) Wait attack until 4 P.M. tomorrow. (3) If don't attack, attack them.

Hancock: (1) Rectify position without moving so as to give up field. (2) Not attack unless our communications are cut. (3) Can't wait long; can't be idle.

Sedgwick: (1) Remain. (2) Wait attack. (3) At least one day.

Slocum: (1) Stay and fight it out.

The unanimous opinion of the council was to stay and await attack. Just as the council broke up, General Meade said to Gibbon, "If Lee attacks tomorrow, it will be on your front. He has made attacks on both our flanks and failed, and if he concludes to try it again it will be on our center." The attack of Lee on the 3rd was made where Meade expected.

During the forenoon of the third day, conditions at headquarters were generally quiet. In the afternoon, when the Confederate artillery on Seminary Ridge opened fire as a prelude to Pickett's Charge, it was directed mainly against the left center of the Union line on Cemetery Ridge. As the location of Meade's headquarters was in the immediate rear, just under the crest of the ridge, much damage was done by the hail of shot and shell that crossed the ridge. A shell exploded in the yard among the staff officers' horses tied to the fence, and a number of them were killed, while still other horses were killed in

the rear of the building. Several members of the headquarters' guard were slightly wounded.

George G. Meade, a grandson of General Meade, in his interesting narrative "With Meade at Gettysburg," tells the following story:

"During this rain of Confederate shell, and while Meade, deep in thought, was walking up and down this little back yard between the house and the Taneytown Road, he chanced to notice that some of his staff, during the enforced inactivity while waiting the pleasure of their general, were gradually and probably unconsciously edging around the side of the house.

" 'Gentlemen,' he said, stopping and smiling pleasantly, 'Are you trying to find a safer place? You remind me of the man who was driving the ox-cart which took ammunition for the heavy guns on the field of Palo Alto. Finding himself within range, he tilted up his cart and got behind it. Just then General Taylor came along, and seeing the attempt at shelter, shouted, "You damned fool; don't you know you are no safer there than anywhere else?" The driver replied, "I don't suppose I am, General, but it kind o' feels so." ' "

As the firing still continued it was decided to move the headquarters several hundred yards south on the Taneytown Road, to a barn on the Cassatt property. There a Confederate shell exploded and wounded General Butterfield, the chief of staff, who was obliged to leave the field and was unable to return that day. After remaining a short time, General Meade and staff removed to General Slocum's headquarters at Power's Hill, along the Baltimore Pike, moving there by way of Granite Lane.

• • • •

THE
LOUISIANA
TIGERS

Major Chatham R. Wheat's battalion of Louisiana Infantry was organized in New Orleans in May, 1861. Their first engagement was in the first battle of Bull Run,

A Union Battery, as in action on the afternoon of the Second Day

Monument of the Irish Brigade.
At the foot of the Celtic Cross
is the Irish wolfhound, sym-
bolic of devotion

John Burns, Gettysburg con-
stable and Mexican War veteran, shouldered his musket
and went out to meet the
Confederates

Spangler's Spring. Used first by the Union, then by the Confederate troops, and since by thousands of tourists. (See page 60)

where Major Wheat was shot through both lungs. After his recovery, he re-entered the service and took an active part in command of the battalion in the defense of Richmond in 1862 against the advance of the Union forces under McClellan. During this campaign the battalion became known as "The Louisiana Tigers" on account of their desperate fighting qualities. At the battle of Gaines Mill, Major Wheat and several other leading officers of the battalion were killed, and the loss of the organization was very heavy. It was then broken up and the survivors distributed among the other Louisiana regiments, of Hays' and Nicholls' brigades of Early's Division of Ewell's Corps. A number of them were in the battle of Gettysburg with these brigades, but not as the separate organization originally known as "The Louisiana Tigers." This designation was given to all the Louisiana troops after the original battalion was discontinued. The story sometimes told, that 1700 Louisiana Tigers attacked East Cemetery Hill on July 2nd, that all but 300 were killed or captured, and that the organization was unknown afterward, is not correct.

. . . .

In the first great battle of the Civil War, at Bull Run, GENERAL there was a bright bay horse with white face and feet. He, MEADE'S as well as his rider, was seriously wounded and the horse "BALDY" was turned back to the quartermaster to recover. In September General Meade bought him and named him "Baldy." Meade became deeply attached to the horse but his staff officers soon began to complain of his peculiar racking gait which was hard to follow. Faster than a walk and slow for a trot, it compelled the staff alternately to trot and walk.

"Baldy" was wounded twice at the first battle of Bull Run; he was at the battle of Drainsville; he took part in two of the seven days' fighting around Richmond in the

summer of 1862; he carried his master at Groveton, August 29th; at the second battle of Bull Run; at South Mountain and at Antietam. In the last battle he was left on the field for dead, but in the next Federal advance he was discovered quietly grazing on the battleground with a deep wound in his neck. He was tenderly cared for and soon was fit for duty. He bore the General at the battles of Fredericksburg and Chancellorsville. For two days he was present at Gettysburg, where he received his most grievous wound from a bullet entering his body between the ribs and lodging there. Meade would not part with him and kept him with the army until the following spring.

In the preparations of the Army of the Potomac for the last campaign, "Baldy" was sent to pasture at Downingtown, Pa. After the surrender of Lee at Appomattox, Meade hurried to Philadelphia where he again met his faithful charger, fully recovered. For many years the horse and the general were inseparable companions, and when Meade died in 1872, "Baldy" followed the hearse. Ten years later he died, and his head and two fore-hoofs were mounted and are now cherished relics of the George G. Meade Post, Grand Army of the Republic, in Philadelphia. • • • •

GENERAL LEE'S "TRAVELLER"   The most famous of the steeds in the stables of General Lee, was "Traveller," an iron-gray horse. He was raised in Greenbriar County, Virginia, near Blue Sulphur Springs, and as a colt won first prize at a fair in Lewisburg. When hostilities commenced, "Traveller," then called "Jeff Davis," was owned by Major Thomas L. Broun, who had paid $175 in gold for him. In the spring of 1862, Lee bought him for $200 and changed his name to "Traveller."

"Traveller" was the especial companion of the general. His fine proportions attracted immediate attention. He was gray in color, with black points, a long mane, and

flowing tail. He stood sixteen hands high, and was five years old in the spring of 1862. His figure was muscular, with deep chest and short back, strong haunches, flat legs, small head, quick eyes, broad forehead, and small feet. His rapid, springy step and bold carriage made him conspicuous. On a long and tedious march he easily carried Lee's weight at five or six miles an hour without faltering and at the end of the day's march seemed to be as fresh as at the beginning. The other horses broke down under the strain and each in turn proved unequal to the rigors of war, but "Traveller" sturdily withstood the hardships of the campaigns in Virginia, Maryland, and Pennsylvania. When, in April, 1865, the last battle of the Army of Northern Virginia had been fought and Lee rode to the McLean House at Appomattox Court House, he was astride "Traveller" who carried him back to his waiting army, and then to Richmond. When Lee became a private citizen and retired to Washington and Lee University as its president, the veteran war-horse was still with him, and as the years passed and both master and servant neared life's ending, they became more closely attached. As the funeral cortege accompanied Lee to his last resting-place, "Traveller" marched behind the hearse. After "Traveller's" death, his skeleton was mounted and is on exhibition at the Lexington (Va.) Military Academy.

"Wheresoever throughout the civilized world the accounts of this great war are read, and down to the latest period of recorded time, in the glorious annals of our common country, there will be no brighter page than that which relates the Battle of Gettysburg."
—EDWARD EVERETT, address at Gettysburg, November 19, 1863.

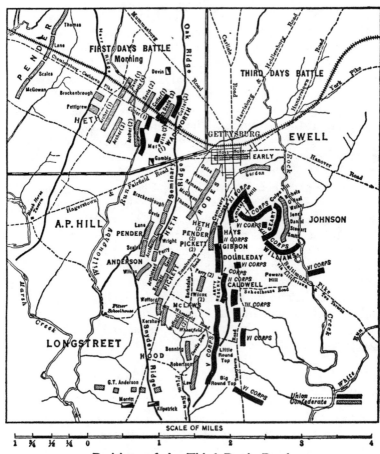

Positions of the Third Day's Battle

CHAPTER VI

THE THIRD DAY'S BATTLE

THE attack and defense of Meade's right continued to its conclusion in the first engagement on the third day. His forces, returning from the left, where they had been sent on the afternoon of the 2nd, found part of their earthworks in possession of the enemy. At daybreak preparations were made to recapture the lost entrenchments. By 10.30 the effort was successful, and Meade's line was once more intact from end to end.

This action on the morning of the 3rd was one of the most hotly contested of the battle. The Confederate losses in killed were almost the same as those of Pickett's Division in the attack on Meade's left center in the afternoon. Meade's losses were comparatively light, as his line was well protected by the line of earthworks. So intense was the artillery and musketry fire that hundreds of trees were shattered. After the repulse, Johnson's forces were withdrawn, and this ended their participation in the battle. SECOND BATTLE AT CULP'S HILL

After the engagement on the morning of the 2nd, the 12th Corps reoccupied its original line, beginning on the right at Spangler's Hill and extending to and over Culp's Hill. Wadsworth's MEADE'S LINE OF THE THIRD DAY

Division of the 1st Corps retained its position of the 2nd, between Culp's Hill and Barlow's Division under Ames of the 11th Corps, at the foot of East Cemetery Hill. Barlow's Division was strengthened by a brigade of the 2nd Corps. Doubleday's Division of the 1st Corps, which had taken the position of Caldwell's Division on the left of the 2nd Corps, remained. Caldwell was posted so as to support the artillery reserve to the left of Doubleday.

The other divisions of the 1st and 2nd Corps remained in the positions they occupied on the morning of the 2nd. The 5th Corps extended the line from the left of the artillery reserve to Big Round Top. Some of the brigades of the 6th Corps were put in position as local reserves and others to protect the flanks of the line. The 3rd Corps was posted in rear of the center as a general reserve. A detachment of cavalry was in reserve in rear of the 2nd Corps at the Angle. Few changes were made in the artillery positions. Beginning at Cemetery Hill and extending to Little Round Top, about ninety guns, under General Hunt, were in position to operate.

LEE'S LINE OF THE THIRD DAY Beginning on the right, Longstreet's Corps held the ground west of Plum Run, including the base of Big Round Top, Devil's Den, and the Peach Orchard. Pickett's Division, after its arrival on the field on the morning of the 3rd, took the place of Anderson in reserve. Heth's

and Pender's Divisions extended the line to the left on Seminary Ridge, connecting with part of Rodes' Division in the western part of the town. Early's and Johnson's Divisions, after the engagement on the morning of the 3rd, held their positions of the 2nd. Changes in the positions of the batteries of artillery were made on the morning of the 3rd. A total of 138 guns were in position to operate. Those on the right were in charge of Colonel E. P. Alexander; those on the left under Colonel R. L. Walker.

After the end of the engagement at Culp's THE BLISS
Hill at 10.30 A.M. there was a short battle for BUILDINGS
the capture of the Bliss house and barn, midway between the lines in front of Ziegler's Grove. These buildings were occupied by Confederate sharpshooters, who were causing considerable loss in Hays' line of the 2nd Corps at the grove. Two regiments were sent forward, the 12th New Jersey and the 14th Connecticut, and the buildings were captured and burned.

Until 1 o'clock there was comparative quiet. THE ARTIL-
It was ended on the stroke of the hour by two LERY DUEL
guns of Miller's battery belonging to the Washington artillery of New Orleans, posted near the Peach Orchard, and fired in rapid succession as a signal to the Confederate artillery.

The Confederate Colonel Alexander says:

"At exactly 1 o'clock by my watch the two signal guns were heard in quick succession. In another

71

minute every gun was at work. The enemy was not slow in coming back at us, and the grand roar of nearly the whole of both armies burst in on the silence.

"The enemy's position seemed to have broken out with guns everywhere, and from Round Top to Cemetery Hill was blazing like a volcano."

The artillery duel was but a preface, intended to clear the ground for the infantry action to follow. The order had already been given by Longstreet to Alexander:

"Colonel: The intention is to advance the infantry if the artillery has the desired effect of driving the enemy off, or having other effect such as to warrant us in making the attack. When the moment arrives advise General Pickett, and of course advance such artillery as you can use in making the attack."

General Wright, who was present when this order was received, expressed doubt as to whether the attack could be successfully made. He said:

"It is not so hard to go there as it looks; I was nearly there with my brigade yesterday. The trouble is to stay there. The whole Yankee army is there in a bunch."

For one and a half hours the air was filled with screaming, whistling shot and shell. An occasional Whitworth missile, from Oak Hill on the north, made, on account of its peculiar form, a noise that could be heard above the din of all others. The headquarters of General Meade at the Leister House formed a concentric

point continually swept with a storm of shot and shell. Headquarters were therefore moved to Slocum's headquarters at Power's Hill, along the Baltimore Pike.

Batteries on the Union line, especially at the Angle, were badly damaged, and General Hunt had others brought forward with additional supplies of ammunition. On the whole the losses inflicted upon the Union infantry were comparatively light. The stone wall and the undulations of the ground afforded protection, as most of the men were lying down.

After the artillery had operated for about an hour and a half, Meade and Hunt deemed it prudent to stop the fire, in order to cool the guns, save ammunition, and allow the atmosphere between the lines to clear of the dense cloud of smoke before the expected attack was made. This pause in the fire led the Confederates to believe that the Union line was demoralized, and that the opportune time had arrived for the onset of the infantry. Accordingly, they moved forward and Pickett's Charge was on.

At the signal station on Little Round Top, General Warren and others saw gray infantry moving out across the plain in front of the Spangler Woods. Warren at once wig-wagged to General Hunt:

"They are moving out to attack."

This message was passed from man to man along the entire Union line.

Pickett's Division of Longstreet's Corps was moved from the rear to the ravine in front of the Spangler Woods and placed in line as follows: Kemper on the right; Garnett on the left in the front line; Armistead in the rear, overlapping Kemper's left and Garnett's right, in the second line. On the left of Garnett was ranged Archer's Brigade of Hill's Corps under Frye, then Pettigrew's Brigade under Marshall. Next to Marshall came Davis' Brigade of Hill's Corps, and on the extreme left Brockenbrough's Brigade, also of Hill's Corps. In the rear of the right of Pickett were the brigades of Wilcox and Perry of Hill's Corps and in the rear of Pettigrew were the brigades of Scales and Lane of Hill's Corps, in command of Trimble.

The column of assault consisted of 42 regiments—19 Virginia, 15 North Carolina, 2 Alabama, 3 Tennessee, and 3 Mississippi—a total of about 15,000 men.

In addition to the artillery fire, they encountered 27 regiments—9 of New York, 5 of Pennsylvania, 3 of Massachusetts, 3 of Vermont, 1 of Michigan, 1 of Maine, 1 of Minnesota, 1 of New Jersey, 1 of Connecticut, 1 of Ohio, and 1 of Delaware—a total of 8,000 to 9,000 men.

In advance of the assaulting column a strong skirmish line was deployed. A skirmish line was

also deployed in front of Meade's line, which fell back as the assaulting column drew near.

General Longstreet ordered General Alexander, Chief of Artillery, to watch the havoc wrought in the Union line and signify the moment for advance. THE AD-VANCE

General Alexander says:

"Before the cannonade opened I made up my mind to give the order to advance within fifteen or twenty minutes after it began. But when I looked at the full development of the enemy's batteries and knew that his infantry was generally protected from fire by stone walls and swells of the ground, I could not bring myself to give the word.

"I let the 15 minutes pass, and 20, and 25, hoping vainly for something to turn up. Then I wrote to Pickett: 'If you are coming at all, come at once, or I cannot give you proper support; but the enemy's fire has not slackened at all; at least eighteen guns are still firing from the cemetery itself.'

"Five minutes after sending that message, the enemy's fire suddenly began to slacken, and the guns in the cemetery limbered up and vacated the position.

"Then I wrote to Pickett: 'Come quick; eighteen guns are gone; unless you advance quick, my ammunition won't let me support you properly.'

"Pickett then rode forward, and on meeting Longstreet said: 'General, shall I advance?' Longstreet nodded his assent and the column moved forward."

The column passed through the line of guns, fifteen or eighteen of which had been ordered to follow. Meanwhile the eighteen Union guns that were withdrawn were replaced by others. The

Union line was once more intact, and it opened a terrific fire against the rapidly moving columns of assault. As the Confederates continued to advance, their courage unaffected in face of the tremendous fire of both artillery and infantry, their enemies were filled with admiration.

At the Emmitsburg Road, where post-and-rail fences had to be crossed, the line was broken, but only for a moment. The musketry fire from the Union line was so heavy that the attacking column was unable to maintain a regular alignment, and when the Angle was reached the identity of the different brigades was lost.

Armistead's Brigade forged to the front at the Angle, and, reaching the wall, Armistead raised his hat on his sword and said:

"Give them the cold steel, boys!"

With a few men he advanced to Cushing's guns, where he fell, mortally wounded. Cushing also was mortally wounded. Garnett, who was mounted, was killed a short distance from the wall. Kemper was badly wounded. Pickett lost all of his field officers but one. The Union Generals Hancock and Gibbon were wounded at the same time. For a short time the struggle was hand to hand.

To the right of the Angle most of the brigades on Pickett's left reached the stone wall on Hays' front at Ziegler's Grove, but were obliged to

retreat after meeting a withering fire both in front and on flank.

The brigades of Wilcox and Perry, in the rear of Pickett's right, did not move until after the advance lines were part way across. Because of a misunderstanding, a gap was opened between Pickett's right and Wilcox's left. At once Stannard's Vermont Brigade of the 1st Corps attacked both Pickett's right and Wilcox's left.

General Pickett, who had reached the Codori buildings, saw that the assaulting forces were unable to accomplish the object of the charge, and ordered a retreat. It was accomplished, but with heavy losses.

Both commanding officers witnessed the retreat: General Meade from where his statue stands east of the Angle, and General Lee from the position of his statue north of the Spangler Woods.

While Pickett's Charge was under way, the ENGAGE-MENTS ON THE UNION LEFT Pennsylvania Reserves, under McCandless, charged from the stone wall on the east side of the Wheatfield and regained possession of Devil's Den and adjacent territory held by Longstreet's forces since the engagement of the afternoon of the 2nd. Farther south, between Big Round Top and the line held by Longstreet's right, a cavalry charge was made by Farnsworth's Brigade of Kilpatrick's Division. Farnsworth was killed. Merritt's Brigade of Buford's Divi-

sion, which reached the field on the 3rd, engaged some of Longstreet's troops along the Emmitsburg Road. The accomplished object of these movements was to prevent Longstreet from giving assistance to the charge of Pickett on Meade's center.

THE CAV-
ALRY FIGHT
ON THE
RIGHT
FLANK

As already noted, General Stuart in his movement in rear of the Army of the Potomac with three brigades of cavalry—Fitzhugh Lee's, Wade Hampton's, and Chambliss'—reached Hanover on June 30th, fought a battle in the streets, and moved on to Carlisle on the afternoon of July 1st. There he got in touch with the main Confederate Army, with which he had been out of communication for seven days.

After an encounter with a portion of Kilpatrick's forces at Hunterstown on the afternoon of July 2nd, he moved up to a position between the Hunterstown and Harrisburg roads on Ewell's left, expecting to reach Meade's rear about the time of Pickett's Charge on Meade's front. He was joined by Jenkins' Confederate Brigade of mounted infantry armed with Enfield rifles. Jenkins was wounded at Hunterstown, and the brigade and the command fell to Colonel Ferguson.

General Gregg, in command of the 2nd Cavalry Division of the Union Army, reached the field east of Gettysburg at the intersection of the Hanover and Low Dutch roads at 11 A.M.

on July 2nd. In the afternoon he halted a movement of Walker's Brigade of Johnson's Division, Ewell's Corps, in their movement from Brinkerhoff Ridge to assist in the attack on Meade's right at Culp's Hill. He bivouacked for the night near the bridge across White Run. On the morning of the 3rd he returned to the position of the 2nd, and took an active part in the cavalry fight on the right flank at the time of Pickett's Charge. In the afternoon, in the important engagement on East Cavalry Field he successfully opposed General Stuart in his efforts to get behind the Union line.

East Cavalry Field is 3 miles east of Gettysburg and includes the territory lying between the York Pike on the north and the Hanover Road on the south. On the east it is bounded by the Low Dutch Road which intersects the Baltimore Pike at its southern end, and the York Pike at its northern end. Brinkerhoff Ridge, which crosses the Hanover Road at right angles about 1½ miles east of the town, forms its boundary on the west. Cress Ridge is formed by the elevation between Cress's Run on the west and Little's Run on the east. Both ridges cross the Hanover Road at a right angle.

All the positions held by troops have been marked and the entire field is readily accessible over well-built roads and avenues. Because of its partial isolation from the principal fields,

THE LOCATION

this important area is not visited as frequently as it should be.

General Stuart did not wish to bring on a general engagement. He expected his skirmishers to keep the Union Cavalry engaged while his other forces were moving undiscovered toward the rear of Meade's line. He says in his report:

"On the morning of July 3, pursuant to instructions from the commanding general, I moved forward to a position to the left of Gen. Ewell's left, and in advance of it, where a commanding ridge (Cress Ridge) completely controlled a wide plain of cultivated fields stretching toward Hanover, on the left, and reaching to the base of the mountain spurs, among which the enemy held position. My command was increased by the addition of Jenkins' Brigade, who here in the presence of the enemy allowed themselves to be supplied with but 10 rounds of ammunition, although armed with approved Enfield muskets.

"I moved this command and W. H. F. Lee's secretly through the woods to a position, and hoped to effect a surprise upon the enemy's rear, but Hampton's and Fitz Lee's Brigades, which had been ordered to follow me, unfortunately debouched into the open ground, disclosing the movement, and causing a corresponding movement of a large force of the enemy's cavalry."

It was the advance of Hampton and Fitzhugh Lee which caused Stuart's plans to miscarry.

On the Union side, General D. McM. Gregg had under his command three brigades of cavalry—one in command of General George A. Custer, who later was responsible for "Custer's

Meade's Headquarters. The Leister House, General Meade's headquarters until the artillery fire on the Third Day compelled him to move. (See page 72)

Devil's Den. Hid among the rocks of Devil's Den, Confederate sharpshooters picked off officers and men occupying Little Round Top. (See page 77)

East Cemetery Hill. Here, on the afternoon of the First Day, General Hancock took command of the Union troops. On the Second Day the guns pointed downward to meet the onslaught of the Confederates

Whitworth Guns. These two Whitworths, imported from England by the Confederates, were the only breech-loading guns used in the battle. (See page 116)

Last Charge" in Indian warfare. General Gregg's report gives a brief description of the many charges and countercharges:

"A strong line of skirmishers displayed by the enemy was evidence that the enemy's cavalry had gained our right, and were about to attack, with the view of gaining the rear of our line of battle. The importance of successfully resisting an attack at this point, which, if succeeded in by the enemy, would have been productive of the most serious consequences, determined me to retain the brigade of the Third Division until the enemy were driven back. General Custer, commanding the brigade, fully satisfied of the intended attack, was well pleased to remain with his brigade. The First New Jersey Cavalry was posted as mounted skirmishers to the right and front in a wood. The Third Pennsylvania Cavalry deployed as dismounted skirmishers to the left and front in open fields, and the First Maryland on the Hanover turnpike, in position to protect the right of my line.

"The very superior force of dismounted skirmishers of the enemy advanced on our left and front required the line to be re-enforced by one of General Custer's regiments. At this time the skirmishing became very brisk on both sides, and the artillery fire was begun by the enemy and ourselves. During the skirmish of the dismounted men, the enemy brought upon the field a column for a charge. The charge of this column was met by the Seventh Michigan Cavalry, of the First (Second) Brigade, Third Division, but not successfully. The advantage gained in this charge was soon wrested from the enemy by the gallant charge of the First Michigan, of the same brigade. This regiment drove the enemy back to his starting point, the enemy with-

drew to his left, and on passing the wood in which the First New Jersey Cavalry was posted, that regiment gallantly and successfully charged the flank of his column. Heavy skirmishing was still maintained by the Third Pennsylvania Cavalry with the enemy, and was continued until nightfall. During the engagement, a portion of this regiment made a very handsome and successful charge upon one of the enemy's regiments. The enemy retired his column behind his artillery, and at dark withdrew from his former position. The fire of the artillery during this engagement was the most accurate that I have ever seen."

Stuart's forces numbered about 7,000, and Gregg and Custer's about 5,000.

LEE'S RETREAT

On the night of the 3rd, Lee withdrew all his forces to Seminary and Snyder ridges. Orders were issued and instructions given for the retreat to the Potomac River at Williamsport and Falling Waters. The effectives moved to Fairfield over the Hagerstown or Fairfield Road. The wagon-train, 17 miles long, with the wounded, was moved by way of the Cashtown Road (Chambersburg Pike), under the command of Brigadier-General John D. Imboden, who has described his interview with General Lee at his headquarters, which were still located in an orchard in the rear of the Seminary buildings, as follows:

"He invited me into his tent, and as soon as we were seated he remarked: 'We must now return to Virginia. As many of our poor wounded as possible must be

taken home. I have sent for you because your men and horses are fresh and in good condition, to guard and conduct our train back to Virginia. The duty will be arduous, responsible, and dangerous, for I am afraid you will be harassed by the enemy's cavalry. I can spare you as much artillery as you may require but no other troops, as I shall need all I have to return safely by a different and shorter route than yours. The batteries are generally short of ammunition, but you will probably meet a supply I have ordered from Winchester to Williamsport.' "

On account of a terrific rainstorm shortly after noon on the 4th there was considerable delay in getting the Confederate train started. Well guarded in front and rear, the head of the column near Cashtown was put in motion and began the ascent of the mountain. The wounded suffered indescribable hardships. Many had been without food for thirty-six hours, and had received no medical attention since the battle. Among the wounded officers were General Pender and General Scales. The trip cost Pender his life. General Imboden said:

"During this retreat I witnessed the most heartrending scenes of the War."

As a military movement the retreat was a success. Though harassed by pursuing forces, the train reached the Potomac with comparatively little loss.

The main Confederate Army crossed the mountain, principally at the Fairfield gap. On

account of the heavy rain, Ewell's Corps, which brought up the rear, did not leave Gettysburg until the forenoon of the 5th. Somewhat delayed, but not seriously impeded, Lee arrived at the Potomac on July 12, finding it too high to cross. There he entrenched his army. The next day, the waters having fallen, he got safely away.

NO PURSUIT BY MEADE

Because of Lee's strong position, Meade made no countercharge. He had won a notable victory, and believed it unwise to risk undoing his work. His army had suffered heavily. Both armies moved south. The Confederate cause had received a severe blow. The defeat at Gettysburg and the surrender of Vicksburg on July 4th to Grant ended all hope of foreign recognition. Yet, for almost two years the desperate struggle was to continue!

THE GETTYSBURG CARNAGE

The War records estimate the Union casualties, killed, wounded, and missing, at 23,000 of the 84,000 engaged. The Confederate casualties are estimated at over 20,000 of the 75,000 engaged. Approximately 10,000 bodies were left at Gettysburg for burial, and 21,000 living men to be healed of their wounds.

No words can picture the desolation of the little town. As the soldiers marched away, their places were taken by physicians and surgeons, nurses and orderlies, civilian as well as military, and the ministrations of mercy began. In these

the citizens of Gettysburg, especially the women, took an important part. Hither came also a new army of parents and wives and brothers and sisters, seeking, sometimes with success, sometimes with grievous disappointment, for their beloved.

. . . .

ENLISTMENTS IN THE UNION ARMY 1861–65, 2,778,309

10 years and under..........25	17 years and under 844,891
11 years and under..........38	18 years and under.....1,151,438
12 years and under..........225	21 years and under.....2,159,798
13 years and under..........300	22 years and older........618,511
14 years and under.........1,525	25 years and older.........46,626
15 years and under 104,987	44 years and older........16,071
16 years and under 231,051	

The total was 2,778,309; allowing for duplicates, members of the three-months, six-months, and one-year regiments re-enlisting for further terms, the total number of individuals in the army was about 2,250,000. The boys under the age of 14 were mainly drummers, but many of them followed the line of battle, doing their duty bravely, and eventually took their places in the ranks.

THE HUMISTON CHILDREN

After the battle there was found on the lot opposite St. James Lutheran Church the body of a Union soldier who held in his hands the ferrotype of three lovely children. A copy of a newspaper containing a description of the picture found its way to a little town in western New York. The affecting tale was told throughout the village, and a lady carried the paper to a friend who had not heard from her husband since the battle. The narrative recalled with dread accuracy a picture which she had sent her husband. Thus did she learn that she was a widow and that her children were fatherless. The name of the soldier was Amos Humiston, Sergeant, 154th New York Volunteers. He is buried in the National Cemetery at Gettysburg.

GETTYSBURG AND WATERLOO

"There are striking points of resemblance between the battlefields of Gettysburg and of Waterloo. On both, the hostile armies were drawn up on two parallel ridges, separated by a shallow valley about three-quarters of a mile wide. The Union salient at the Peach Orchard, occupied by Sickles on the Second Day, corresponds to the farm of Hougomont, held by the British at Waterloo. The Codori buildings, near the center of the field, are similar to the farm of La Haie-Sainte.

"The chief point of dissimilarity is that the main highway at Waterloo ran perpendicular to the two lines of battle, while at Gettysburg the Emmitsburg Road was nearly parallel to the lines. This road was bordered on either side by a five-rail post-fence which proved almost as formidable an obstacle to the charge of Pickett's men as did the 'sunken road' at Waterloo to the assaults of Napoleon's Old Guard. When the Confederates reached these fences, they were forced to climb over, under a heavy short-range musketry fire, before advancing."

86

CHAPTER VII

HAPPENINGS ON THE THIRD DAY

O N the afternoon of July 3rd, Captain William E. A MEDAL
Miller, of Company H, 2nd Brigade, of Gregg's FOR DIS-
Division of Union Cavalry, made a charge against the OBEDIENCE
Confederate Cavalry, in command of Major-General
J. E. B. Stuart, in their movement from Cress Ridge,
East Cavalry Field, to reach the rear of Meade's line at
the time of Pickett's Charge.

The incident is described by Captain William Brooke
Rawle, a participant in the charge, in his "History of the
Third Pennsylvania Cavalry."

"When the cavalry fighting began, Captain Miller's
squadron was stationed in Lott's woods to the west of
the Low Dutch Road, beyond the Hanover Road, and
was deployed, mounted as skirmishers, along the western
edge of the woods. There was considerable long-range
firing before the climax of the fighting came. About
3 o'clock in the afternoon . . . a large body of cavalry,
which proved to be Hampton's and Fitzhugh Lee's
brigades, was seen approaching in magnificent order,
mounted, from the northern side of the field. Captain
Miller and I rode out a few yards in front of our position
to a slight rise in the ground to get a good view. The
enemy quickened his pace, first to a trot, then to a gallop,
and then the charge was sounded. The nearest available
compact body of Union Cavalry at hand to meet the
enemy was the 1st Michigan Cavalry of General Custer's
Brigade, which was serving temporarily under General
Gregg. It was ordered to meet the enemy's charge by a
counter-charge, although the Confederate brigade greatly
outnumbered the Michigan regiment. Captain Miller and

I saw at once that unless more men were sent against the enemy the Michigan regiment would be swept from the field. He said to me, 'I have been ordered to hold this position at all hazards, but if you will back me up if I get into trouble for exceeding my orders, I will make a charge with the squadron.' This was in order to make a diversion in favor of our troops, and help the Michigan men. I assured him in an emphatic manner that I would stand by him through thick and thin. He then ordered me to rally the left wing of the squadron while he did the same with the right. When this was done the squadron fired a volley into the Confederate column, which was within easy range. The men were very impatient to begin their charge, and the right wing, headed by Captain Miller, started off at a gallop.

"A stone and rail fence divided the line of the squadron front, running at right angles to it, and I had to make a slight detour to get around it with the left wing of the squadron. This, and the fact that the head of the squadron was headed to the right oblique, caused a gap of some thirty yards or so between the rear of the portion of the squadron under Captain Miller and myself with the left of the left portion. Meanwhile the two opposing columns had met, and the head of the Confederate column was fast becoming jammed, and the men on the flanks were beginning to turn back. Captain Miller, with his men struck the left flank of the enemy's column pretty well towards the rear, about two-thirds or three-fourths of the way down, and as the impetus of the latter had stopped while his men had full headway on, he drove well into the column and cut off its rear and forced it back in the direction whence it came, and the captain and some of his men got as far as the Rummel house. As to this last, I learned from the men engaged. Captain Miller was wounded in the arm during the fight.

"I myself with the rear portion of Captain Miller's squadron did not succeed in getting all the way through. Just as I and my men reached the flank of the enemy many of the latter were getting to the rear and we were swept along with the current and scattered, some of us, including myself, though narrowly escaping capture, succeeding in working our way in one's and two's to the right, where we got back into our lines again.

"The gallant conduct and dashing charge made by Captain Miller and his men were commented upon by all who saw it. A fact that made it all the more commendable was that it was done upon his own responsibility, without orders from a superior officer."

In July, 1897, a Congressional Medal of Honor was bestowed upon Captain Miller by direction of President McKinley, through the Secretary of War, General Russell A. Alger. The conferring of this tribute was especially appropriate, inasmuch as General Alger himself had participated on the right flank as the Colonel of the 5th Michigan, and was therefore eminently competent to decide.

. . . .

THE WENTZ HOUSE

The Wentz house, which stands at the intersection of the Emmitsburg and Wheatfield roads, is now a Government-owned property, and is marked with an iron tablet with the inscription "Wentz House." It is not the house that was there at the time of the battle; the original building was dismantled and the present building erected on the same site.

At the time of the battle the house was owned and occupied by John Wentz, who cultivated the small tract of land belonging to it. He was twice married, and at this time was living with his second wife, who was the mother of Henry Wentz, the principal actor in an interesting incident of the battle of Gettysburg.

For many years before the beginning of the Civil War, carriage and coach-building was one of the leading industries of Gettysburg. Henry Wentz served an apprenticeship with the Ziegler firm of Gettysburg. He was frequently sent to deliver the products of the firm, and thereby became well acquainted with the different sections where sales were made.

In the early '50's he decided to move to Martinsburg, Va. (now W. Va.), and establish a carriage-building shop of his own. When a local military organization was formed and designated the "Martinsburg Blues," Henry became a member. Equipped with uniforms and arms, the members were drilled from time to time. Similar organizations were formed throughout the North as well as the South. Most of the members of the Martinsburg Blues, including Henry Wentz, decided to cast their lot with the Southern cause, and were assigned to places in the armies of the South. But, by the irony of fate, he was destined to get back to his old home and command a battery posted back of the house on his father's land.

During the first day the Wentz property was not in danger, but when General Lee extended his line of battle south along the line of Seminary Ridge, and General Meade prolonged his line opposite on Cemetery Ridge in preparation for the battle of the second day, the Wentz family, with the exception of the father, decided to seek a safer location. On the night of the second day, after Sickles' advanced line at the Wentz house had been repulsed and occupied by the forces under General Lee, Henry Wentz visited his old home and was greatly surprised to find his father still there.

Early in the morning of the third day, 75 guns, in command of Colonel E. P. Alexander, were moved forward from Lee's first line to the line held by Sickles' advanced line on the second day. The battery in charge of Henry

Wentz, who held the rank of lieutenant, was posted back of his old home, and he took an active part in the terrific artillery engagement prior to Pickett's Charge that ended on that part of the field. Henry's father kept to the cellar and, singularly, passed through it all unharmed.

After the repulse of Pickett's Charge, the guns were withdrawn to their first line. During the night of the third day, Henry was anxious to know whether or not his father was still safe. He therefore went over to the house and found him fast asleep and unhurt in a corner of the cellar. Not wishing to disturb his much-needed rest, he found the stump of a candle, lit it, and wrote, "Good-bye and God bless you!" This message he pinned on the lapel of his father's coat and returned to his command preparatory to the retreat to Virginia.

Early on the morning of the 4th, the father awoke from his much-needed sleep and found that all the soldiers had departed. He then walked back to the ridge and saw Lee's army making hurried preparations for the retreat.

. . . .

At the battle of Gettysburg the 13th Vermont was a part of General Stannard's Vermont command. The 2nd Vermont Brigade had been left on outpost duty in Virginia until the third day after the Army of the Potomac had passed in pursuit of Lee's troops into Maryland and Pennsylvania. Then the brigade got orders to proceed by forced marches to join the Army of the Potomac. The latter was also on a forced march, but in six days' time the Vermonters had overtaken the main body. Just before the first day's battle, Captain Brown's command came up to a well at which was an armed guard. "You can't get water here," said the guard. "'Gainst orders." "Damn your orders!" said Captain Brown, and then with all the canteens of the men, and with only one man to help him,

FOUGHT WITH A HATCHET

he thrust the guard aside and filled the canteens. His arrest followed, and he was deprived of his sword.

When the battle began, Captain Brown was a prisoner. He begged for a chance to rejoin his company, and was allowed to go. His men were far away at the front, and he had no weapons. He picked up a camp hatchet and ran all the way to the firing-line, reached it, rushed into the fray, and singling out a Rebel officer 50 yards away, penetrated the Rebel ranks, collared the officer, wresting from him his sword and pistol, after which he dropped the hatchet, while his men cheered him.

When the design for the 13th Vermont monument was made, it was the desire of the committee to have the statue represent Captain Brown, hatchet in hand. Accordingly, a model was prepared, but the Federal Government would not permit its erection. A second model was approved, showing Captain Brown holding a sabre and belt in his hand, the hatchet lying at his feet as though just dropped. The sabre depicted in the statue is an exact reproduction of the one captured.

This monument is on the east side of Hancock Avenue, near the large Stannard monument.

. . . .

AFTER THE BATTLE   This is an extract from "Four Years with the Army of the Potomac," by Brigadier-General Regis de Trobriand, who commanded a brigade of Birney's Division of the 3rd Corps during the battle of Gettysburg:

"Between eight and nine o'clock in the evening of the 3rd, as the last glimmers of daylight disappeared behind us, I received an order to go down into the flat, and occupy the field of battle with two brigades in line. That of Colonel Madill was added to mine for that purpose. General Ward, who temporarily commanded the Division, remained in reserve with the 3rd.

"The most profound calm reigned now, where a few hours before so furious a tempest had raged. The moon, with her smiling face, mounted up in the starry heavens as at Chancellorsville. Her pale light shone equally upon the living and the dead, the little flowers blooming in the grass as well as upon the torn bodies lying in the pools of clotted blood. Dead bodies were everywhere. On no field of battle have I ever seen them in such numbers. The greater part of my line was strewn with them, and, when the arms were stacked and the men asleep, one was unable to say, in that mingling of living and dead, which would awake the next morning and which would not.

"Beyond the line of advanced sentinels, the wounded still lay where they had fallen, calling for assistance or asking for water. Their cries died away without any reply in the silence of the night, for the enemy was close by, and it was a dangerous undertaking to risk advancing into the space which separated us. In making an attempt, an officer of my staff drew three shots, which whistled unpleasantly near his ears. All labors of charity were necessarily put off till the next morning. It is sad to think that this was a sentence of death to numbers of the unfortunate. Mournful thoughts did not hinder the tired soldiers from sleeping. Everything was soon forgotten in a dreamless slumber.

"At dawn of day, when I awakened, the first object which struck my eyes was a young sergeant stretched out on his back, his head resting on a flat stone, serving for a pillow. His position was natural, even graceful. One knee slightly raised, his hands crossed on his breast, a smile on his lips, caused by a dream, perhaps, of her who awaited his return in the distant Green Mountains. He was dead. Wounded, he had sought out this spot in which to die. His haversack was near him. He had taken out of it a little book on which his last looks had been cast, for the

book was still open in his stiffened fingers. It was the New Testament; on the first leaf a light hand had traced in pencil, some letters, rubbed out, which one might think were a name. I have kept the volume, and on the white space, to the unknown name I have added, 'Died at Gettysburg, July 3, 1863.'

"During the night, the enemy had drawn back his pickets to the other side of the Emmitsburg Road, and left us free access to assist the wounded. The appearance of litters and ambulance wagons strengthened them, by giving them hope. They related their engagements of the evening before, and their sufferings during the night. One of them, pointing out the dead lying around him, said: 'This one lived only till sundown; that one lasted until about midnight. There is one who was still groaning but an hour ago.'

"Continuing my walk, I came near a large isolated rock. It might have been eight or ten feet high, and fifteen or twenty feet broad. Rounding on the side towards the enemy, but flat as a wall on the opposite side, it had served as an advanced post for one of our companies, probably belonging to Stannard's brigade. What had happened there? Had they been surprised by the rapid advance of the enemy? Had they tried to shelter themselves behind that stone during the fight? Had the firing of canister by our guns rendered retreat impossible? Had they refused to surrender? No one, to my knowledge, escaped to tell. Whatever was the cause, there were twenty lying there cut down by lead and steel, and amongst the pile I recognized the uniform of an officer and the chevrons of a sergeant.

"When I returned to the center of my line, the ambulances were at work, and squads detailed from each regiment picked up the arms which were scattered by thousands over the field. A little later my command was

relieved, and again took its position of the evening before.

"Some reconnaissances sent out to look for the enemy had not far to go to find him. His pickets were still on the edge of the woods in front of the Seminary Heights. We afterwards learned that he expected, during the whole day, that we would attack, hoping to get revenge. But General Meade, content with his victory, would not take the risk of compromising it by leaving his position before Lee had abandoned his, in which he acted wisely, whatever may have been said to the contrary.

"The afternoon was thus spent in first picking up our wounded and afterwards those of the enemy. The ambulance wagons were hardly enough for the work. The litter-bearers placed the wounded along our lines, where they had to await their turn to be taken to the rear. We did what we could to make the delay as short as possible, for many of them were brave Southern boys, some having enlisted because they honestly believed it was their duty, others torn by force from their families, to be embodied in the Rebel army by the inexorable conscription. After the defeat, they were resigned, without boasting, and expressed but one wish: that the war would terminate as soon as possible, since the triumph of the North appeared to be but a question of time.

"I recall to mind a young man from Florida who told me his history. His name was Perkins, and he was scarcely twenty years old. The only son of aged parents, he had in vain endeavored to escape service. Tracked everywhere by the agents of the Richmond government, he had been forced to take up the musket, and had done his duty so well that he had been rapidly promoted to sergeant. In the last charge of the day before, he had had his left heel carried away by a piece of shell, and his right hand shattered by a canister shot. One amputation, at least, probably two, was what he had to expect; and yet he did

not complain. But when he spoke of his aged parents awaiting his return, and of the sad condition in which he would re-enter the paternal home, his smile was more heart-breaking than any complaint. In order that his wounds might be sooner dressed, one of my aids, Lieutenant Houghton, let him have his horse, at the risk of marching on foot if we moved before he was returned.

"The next night we passed in the rain. It always rains on the day after a great battle. On the morning following we discovered the enemy to be in full retreat. Seeing that the attack he expected did not come off, and fearing for the safety of his communications with the Potomac, General Lee could do nothing else but retire through the mountains, which he did during the night of the 4th and 5th of July. Then only began that disorder in his columns, and that confusion, the picture of which has been somewhat exaggerated; an almost inevitable consequence, besides, to that kind of a movement. Our cavalry began to harass him on the flanks, while the 6th Corps, having remained intact, pressed on his rear-guard.

"The difficulties that General Sedgwick met in the Fairfield pass, where the enemy had intrenched, probably made General Meade fear that a direct pursuit would entail too great loss of time in the mountains. So, instead of following Lee in the valley of the Cumberland, he decided to march on a parallel line, to the east of the South Mountains." . . . .

AN HONEST MAN   General E. P. Alexander, Chief of Artillery of Longstreet's Corps, tells of a trade that occurred during the retreat from Gettysburg:

"Near Hagerstown I. had an experience with an old Dunkard which gave me a high and lasting respect for the people of that faith. My scouts had had a horse transaction with this old gentleman, and he came to see

Little Round Top, whose boulder-strewn face was assaulted by
brave Confederates and held by brave Unionists
(See pages 50 and 51)

Little Round Top. Its strategic importance was seen by General
Warren, who, on the afternoon of the Second Day, commanded
it to be fortified and held. (See pages 50 and 141)

General Warren as he appeared on Little Round Top

me about it. He made no complaint, but said it was his only horse, and as the scouts had told him we had some hoof-sore horses we should have to leave behind, he came to ask if I would trade him one of those for his horse, as without one his crop would be lost.

"I recognized the old man at once as a born gentleman in his delicate characterization of the transaction as a trade. I was anxious to make the trade as square as circumstances would permit. So I assented to his taking a foot-sore horse, and offered him besides payment in Confederate money. This he respectfully declined. Considering how the recent battle had gone, I waived argument on the point of its value but tried another suggestion. I told him that we were in Maryland as the guests of the United States; that after our departure the Government would pay all bills left behind; and that I would give him an order on the United States for the value of his horse and have it approved by General Longstreet. To my surprise he declined this also. I supposed then that he was simply ignorant of the bonanza in a claim against the Government, and I explained that; and, telling him that money was no object to us under the circumstances, I offered to include the value of his whole farm. He again said he wanted nothing but the foot-sore horse. Still anxious that the war should not grind this poor old fellow in his poverty, I suggested that he take two or three foot-sore horses which we would have to leave anyhow, when we marched. Then he said, 'Well, sir, I am a Dunkard, and the rule of our church is an eye for an eye, and a tooth for a tooth, and a horse for a horse, and I can't break the rule.'

"I replied that the Lord, who made all horses, knew that a good horse was worth a dozen old battery scrubs; and after some time prevailed on him to take two, by calling one of them a gift. But that night we were awak-

97

ened about midnight by approaching hoofs, and turned out expecting to receive some order. It was my old Dunkard leading one of his foot-sores. 'Well, sir,' he said, 'you made it look all right to me today when you were talking; but after I went to bed tonight I got to thinking it all over, and I don't think I can explain it to the church, and I would rather not try.' With that he tied old foot-sore to a fence and rode off abruptly. Even at this late day it is a relief to my conscience to tender to his sect this recognition of their integrity and honesty, in lieu of the extra horse which I vainly endeavored to throw into the trade. Their virtues should commend them to all financial institutions in search of incorruptible employees."

. . . .

EXTRACTS FROM THE DIARY OF COLONEL FREMANTLE   Colonel Fremantle, a member of the Cold Stream Guards, was a guest of the Army of Northern Virginia during the Gettysburg campaign. After the battle of Gettysburg, he returned to England and published "Three Months in the Southern States." The following is a vivid extract, describing a part of the battle from the Confederate lines.

"*July 1st (Wednesday)*. At 4.30 P.M. we came in sight of Gettysburg, and joined General Lee and General Hill, who were on the top of one of the ridges which form a peculiar feature of the country round Gettysburg. We could see the enemy retreating up one of the opposite ridges, pursued by the Confederates with loud yells. The position into which the enemy had been driven was evidently a strong one. His right appeared to rest on a cemetery, on the top of a high ridge to the right of Gettysburg, as we looked at it.

"General Hill now came up and told me he had been very unwell all day, and in fact he looks very delicate. He said he had two divisions engaged, and had driven

the enemy four miles into the present position, capturing a great many prisoners, some cannon, and some colors. He said, however, that the Yankees had fought with a determination unusual to them.

"*July 2nd* (*Thursday*). At 2 P.M. General Longstreet advised me, if I wished to have a good view of the battle, to return to my tree of yesterday. I did so and remained there with Lawley and Captain Schreibert during the rest of the afternoon. But until 4.45 P.M. all was profoundly quiet, and we began to doubt whether a fight was coming off today at all. At that time, however, Longstreet suddenly commenced a heavy cannonade on the right. Ewell immediately took it up on the left. The enemy replied with equal fury, and in a few moments the firing along the whole line was as heavy as it is possible to conceive. A dense smoke arose for six miles; there was little wind to drive it away, and the air seemed full of shells— each of which appeared to have a different style of going, and made a different noise from the others. The ordnance on both sides is of a very varied description. Every now and then a caisson would blow up—if a Federal one, a Confederate yell would immediately follow. The Southern troops, when charging, or to express their delight, always yell in a manner peculiar to themselves. The Yankee cheer is much like ours, but the Confederate officers declare that the Rebel yell has a particular merit, and always produces a salutary effect upon their adversaries. A corps is sometimes spoken of as 'a good yelling regiment.'

"As soon as the firing began, General Lee joined Hill just below our tree, and he remained there nearly all the time, looking through his field-glasses, sometimes talking to Hill and sometimes to Colonel Long of his staff. But generally he sat quite alone on the stump of a tree. What I remarked especially was, that during the whole time the

firing continued, he sent only one message, and received only one report. It evidently is his system to arrange the plan thoroughly with the three commanders, and then leave to them the duty of modifying and carrying it out to the best of their abilities.

"When the cannonade was at its height, a Confederate band of music, between the cemetery and ourselves, began to play polkas and waltzes, which sounded very curious, accompanied by the hissing and bursting of the shells.

"At 5.45 all became comparatively quiet on our left and in the cemetery; but volleys of musketry on the right told us that Longstreet's infantry were advancing, and the onward progress of the smoke showed that he was progressing favorably; but about 6.30 there seemed to be a check, and even a slight retrograde movement. . . . A little before dark the firing dropped off in every direction, and soon ceased altogether. We then received intelligence that Longstreet had carried everything before him for some time, capturing several batteries and driving the enemy from his positions; but when Hill's Florida brigade and some other troops gave way, he was forced to abandon a small portion of the ground he had won, together with all the captured guns, except three. His troops, however, bivouacked during the night on ground occupied by the enemy in the morning.

"*July 3rd* (*Friday*). At 2.30 P.M., after passing General Lee and his staff, I rode on through the woods in the direction in which I had left Longstreet. I soon began to meet many wounded men returning from the front; many of them asked in piteous tones the way to a doctor or an ambulance. The farther I got, the greater became the number of the wounded. At last I came to a perfect stream of them flocking through the woods in numbers as great as the crowd in Oxford Street in the middle of the

day. Some were walking alone on crutches composed of two rifles, others were supported by men less badly wounded than themselves, and others carried on stretchers by the ambulance corps, but in no case did I see a sound man helping the wounded to the rear unless he carried the red badge of the ambulance corps. They were still under heavy fire, the shells bringing down great limbs of trees, and carrying further destruction amongst this melancholy procession. I saw all this in much less time than it takes to write it, and although astonished to meet such vast numbers of wounded, I had not seen enough to give me any idea of the real extent of the mischief.

"When I got close up to General Longstreet, I saw one of his regiments advancing through the woods in good order; so, thinking I was just in time to see the attack, I remarked to the General that 'I wouldn't have missed this for anything.' Longstreet was seated at the top of a snake fence at the edge of the woods (Spangler Woods), and looking perfectly calm and imperturbed. He replied, laughing, 'The devil you wouldn't! I would like to have missed it very much; we've attacked and been repulsed: look there!'

"For the first time I then had a view of the open space between the two positions, and saw it covered with Confederates slowly and sulkily returning towards us in small broken parties, under a heavy fire of artillery. But the fire where we were was not so bad as farther to the rear; for although the air seemed alive with shells, yet the greater number burst behind us. The General told me that Pickett's Division had succeeded in carrying the enemy's position and captured his guns, but after remaining there twenty minutes, it had been forced to retire on the retreat of Heth and Pettigrew on his left. . . . .

"Major Walton was the only officer with him (Longstreet) when I came up—all the rest had been put in the

charge. In a few minutes Major Latrobe arrived on foot, carrying his saddle, having just had his horse killed. Colonel Sorrell was also in the same predicament, and Captain Goree's horse was wounded in the mouth. . . .

"Soon after I joined General Lee, who had in the meanwhile come to that part of the field on becoming aware of the disaster. If Longstreet's conduct was admirable, that of General Lee was perfectly sublime. He was engaged in rallying and in encouraging the broken troops, and was riding about a little in front of the woods, quite alone—the whole of his staff being engaged in a similar manner farther to the rear. His face, which is always placid and cheerful, did not show signs of the slightest disappointment or annoyance; and he was addressing to every soldier he met a few words of encouragement, such as, 'All this will come right in the end: we'll talk it over afterwards; but, in the meantime, all good men must rally. We want all good and true men just now.' He spoke to all the wounded men that passed him, and the slightly wounded he exhorted 'to bind up their hurts and take up a musket' in this emergency. Very few failed to answer his appeal, and I saw many badly wounded men take off their hats and cheer him. He said to me, 'This has been a sad day for us, Colonel—a sad day; but we can't expect always to gain victories.' He was also kind enough to advise me to get into some more sheltered position. . . .

"I saw General Wilcox come up to him, and explain, almost crying, the state of his brigade. General Lee immediately shook hands with him and said cheerfully, 'Never mind, General, all this has been *my* fault—it is I that have lost this fight, and you must help me out of it in the best way you can.' In this manner I saw General Lee encourage and reanimate his somewhat dispirited troops, and magnanimously take upon his own shoulders the whole weight of the repulse."

CHAPTER VIII

THE CAVALRY

CAVALRY has been well named "the eye of the army," since without it all movements are made in the dark. In the Battle of Gettysburg the Union cavalry was more actively engaged than the Confederate, the latter taking no part until the afternoon of the third day, when the opposing forces met on the Rummel Farm in the greatest cavalry battle of the war.

The Union cavalry consisted of a corps of three divisions, each composed of three brigades, except the last which had but two brigades. The corps was commanded by Major-General Alfred Pleasonton. The commander of the 1st Division was Brigadier-General John Buford. Brigadier-General David McM. Gregg was in command of the 2nd, and his brigades were commanded by Colonels John B. McIntosh, Pennock Huey, and J. Irvin Gregg. The 3rd Division commander was Brigadier-General Judson Kilpatrick; his two brigades were in command of Brigadier-Generals Elon J. Farnsworth and George A. Custer. UNION CAVALRY

The Confederate cavalry consisted of one division under Major-General J. E. B. Stuart, and was composed of seven brigades, commanded by Brigadier-Generals Wade Hampton, Beverly CONFEDERATE CAVALRY

H. Robertson, Fitzhugh Lee, W. H. F. Lee (John R. Chambliss), William E. Jones, Albert G. Jenkins, and John D. Imboden.

When Lee began his invasion of the North, Jenkins' Brigade moved in advance of the infantry and was the first to cross the Potomac, reaching, eventually, Oyster Point, on the right bank of the Susquehanna opposite Harrisburg, the most northern point of the invasion. Imboden's Brigade moved farther west, in the vicinity of Romney, W. Va., and Cumberland, Md., and did not reach the field at Gettysburg until the battle had about ended. The other five brigades guarded the gaps along the Blue Ridge as the army moved toward the Potomac.

UNION ADVANCE

When Meade moved the Union Army from the vicinity of Frederick, Md., to Pipe Creek, where he established a tentative line of battle, Gregg's Division of cavalry guarded the right, Buford the left, and Kilpatrick the center. Buford, with Gamble's and Devin's brigades, reached Gettysburg from Emmitsburg on June 30th. Merritt's Brigade was left at Emmitsburg to guard the rear, and did not get here until the afternoon of July 3rd. Buford, on his arrival, sent out scouts on all the roads to watch and report the movements of the enemy.

CONFEDER-ATE ADVANCE

When Buford arrived at Gettysburg on June 30th, Pettigrew's Brigade of Hill's Confederate Corps of infantry was on its way from

Cashtown to get supplies. Seeing the approach of Buford's troopers, Pettigrew withdrew after reaching Seminary Ridge, as he did not wish to bring on a battle at once. On the morning of July 1st, Hill sent the divisions of Heth and Pender from Cashtown on a reconnaissance in force. This movement of Hill was met by Buford's skirmishers, and the opening shot of the Battle of Gettysburg was a carbine-shot fired at Hill's advance when it reached the ridge west of Marsh Creek, on the Cashtown Pike.

THE FIRST DAY

While his skirmishers were delaying Hill's advance, Buford deployed Gamble's Brigade, dismounted, along the line of Willoughby's Run south of the Cashtown Pike, and Devin's Brigade north of the pike on Oak Ridge, reaching to the Mummasburg road. Calef's battery of horse artillery, attached to the division, was posted on both sides of the pike north of McPherson Woods, now known as Reynolds Grove. With this force of about 3,200 Buford checked the advance of Hill's veterans for over two hours, anxiously watching and waiting meanwhile for the arrival of Reynolds with the 1st Corps of Union infantry. At 10 A.M. a part of the corps arrived and Buford was relieved. Gamble was moved to the left near the Hagerstown road.

When the 1st Corps was compelled to withdraw to Cemetery Hill, Gamble helped to cover the retreat. On the approach of Rodes' Confederate infantry on the Carlisle road, Devin's Brigade was moved to the right of the Harrisburg road and thus successfully covered the retreat of the 11th Corps.

Buford's initial fight made Gettysburg the battlefield, and without it it is doubtful whether there would have been a second and third day's conflict.

THE SECOND DAY

Until about 11 o'clock of the second day, Buford's Cavalry patrolled the field between Seminary Ridge on the west and Cemetery Ridge on the east.

On account of a misunderstanding, Buford was then ordered by Meade to move to West-minster, Md., to refit and to guard the supplies. Meade was led to believe that Gregg's Division would arrive before the departure of Buford, but it unfortunately came too late to be of service as a patrol.

In the evening, Gregg halted the movement of Walker's Brigade of infantry on Brinkerhoff Ridge, 2 miles east of the town, on its way to assist Johnson in his attack on the Union right at Culp's Hill. With this exception there was no cavalry battle on any part of the field.

THE THIRD DAY

For an account of this important engagement the reader is referred to pages 78 to 82 of the account of the battle.

The final charge was, perhaps, the most spectacular of the whole battle. Stuart was still hopeful that by making a mass attack he could win his way through to the rear of Meade's line and cause a panic while Pickett was moving against the front.

Following a brief lull at about three o'clock, the brigades of Hampton and Fitzhugh Lee moved out from a screen of woodland and formed their line for a last effort. With sabres drawn and glistening in the sunlight, they moved forward. The magnificent sight called forth many expressions of admiration from their opponents. At once, Gregg's Union artillery opened with shell and shrapnel, tearing gaps in the ranks of the advancing column. Gregg's soldiers rode forward, first at a trot, but soon quickened their pace to a gallop. So sudden and violent was the collision that many of the horses were turned end over end and crushed their riders beneath them. The clashing of sabres, the firing of pistols, the demands for surrender, and the yells of the combatants filled the air. Charge and countercharge was made as the columns wavered back and forth. Gregg ordered Custer to lead the 1st Michigan and move in. Hampton was

wounded by a sabre cut on the head, and his gallant troopers began to waver and fall back. Fitzhugh Lee was also compelled to retreat, and soon the struggle ended. Some skirmishing and artillery firing was kept up until dark, then Stuart returned to the York Pike and prepared to guard the retreat of Lee's Army to the Potomac. The casualties of Stuart's forces numbered 240. The report of Gregg's Division, including Custer's Brigade, shows a total loss of 254.

Mr. Rummel, the owner of part of the cavalry field, who assisted in removing the dead, found a Unionist and a Confederate who had cut each other down with their sabres, lying with their feet together, their heads in opposite directions, and the blood-stained sabre of each still tight in his grip. At another point he found a Virginian and a Pennsylvanian who fought on horseback with their sabres until they finally clinched and their horses ran from under them. Their heads and shoulders were severely cut, and their fingers, though stiff in death, were so firmly imbedded in each other's flesh that they could not be removed without the aid of force.

CAVALRY SOUTH OF MEADE'S LEFT

When the engagement between the cavalry of Gregg and Stuart was about over, Farnsworth's Brigade of Kilpatrick's Division, by order of Kilpatrick, attacked the right of Law's Brigade of Confederate infantry, then holding

the extreme right of Lee's line. The territory over which Farnsworth was ordered to move is unsuited for the operations of mounted troops, being covered with large boulders and stone fences. Farnsworth was confronted by both infantry and artillery but nevertheless made the attack and gave Law some trouble to repel it. Farnsworth was killed on the north slope of Big Round Top.

Merritt's Brigade of Buford's Division had been left at Emmitsburg to guard the rear when Buford moved to Gettysburg on June 30th. Arriving from Emmitsburg on the afternoon of July 3rd, it held a line south of that held by Farnsworth, astride the Emmitsburg road, on territory now known as South Cavalry Field. At the time of Farnsworth's charge against Law, Merritt was engaged with Anderson's Brigade of Confederate infantry. These two attacks by the Union cavalry prevented the Confederate forces engaged from assisting in Pickett's Charge or threatening any other part of Meade's line.

In moving from Emmitsburg on July 3rd, Merritt dispatched one regiment, the 6th U. S. Cavalry, to Fairfield to attack the Confederate trains that were believed to be in that vicinity. The regiment met the cavalry brigades of Jones and Robertson, who covered the rear of Lee's Army, and a most determined battle was fought over fields that were surrounded by high post

fences. The losses were heavy on both sides. This was the last cavalry engagement of the Battle of Gettysburg.

On the night of July 3rd, Lee withdrew his army to Seminary and Snyder ridges, and orders were given for the retreat to the Potomac at Williamsport and Falling Waters. Lee's orders to Stuart were:

> "General Stuart will designate a cavalry command, not exceeding two squadrons, to precede and follow the army in its line of march, the commander of the advance reporting to the commander of the leading corps, the commander of the rear to the commander of the rear corps."

Two roads were selected for retreat, the Fairfield road for the effectives, and the Cashtown road for the wagon train and the wounded. During pouring rain one long Confederate train of wagons moved through Cashtown and another through Fairfield. The cavalry brigades of Hampton and Fitzhugh Lee guarded the rear of the Cashtown train, and Imboden with his brigade the front and flanks. The Fairfield train was practically unguarded. Hill was in the advance, Longstreet next, followed by Ewell, who delayed leaving until the morning of the 5th.

Stuart, with the brigades of Jenkins and W. H. F. Lee, moved round the Confederate Army to Emmitsburg where he learned that Kilpatrick's Union cavalry had preceded him on its way to

Monterey. Believing that Kilpatrick would be halted by Robertson, Stuart moved toward Cavetown, where he found Kilpatrick confronting him.

On the morning of July 6th, Buford's Division was at Frederick, where Meade established his headquarters on the 7th, after moving from Gettysburg. Buford left Frederick on the 6th on his way to Williamsport. J. I. Gregg's Brigade of Gregg's Division followed Imboden's train through Cashtown to Greencastle but was prevented from attacking by Fitzhugh Lee's Brigade. McIntosh's Brigade of Gregg's Division followed the Confederate Army through Monterey Gap. Unable to cross the Potomac on account of high water, Lee established a line of battle. As the river protected his right flank, Stuart's Cavalry was united on the left flank. On reaching the Potomac, Meade took up a position in front of Lee's line, with Kilpatrick's Cavalry on the right, Buford's on the left, and Gregg's Division at Boonsboro in reserve. On the night of July 13th, Lee recrossed the Potomac, and this ended the engagements north of the river.

"Gettysburg will ever be preëminently the most renowned of all the battles of the war for the Union, not only because of its magnitude and immediate results, but also by reason of the grave consequences dependent upon the issue."

—J. M. VANDERSLICE

COLONEL JOHN P. NICHOLSON

Colonel John Page Nicholson was born in Philadelphia on July 4, 1842, and died in the same city on March 22, 1922. He enlisted in Company K, 28th Infantry, Pennsylvania Volunteers, June 30, 1861, and became sergeant and commissary sergeant in July of the same year, and subsequently quartermaster of the regiment. He was brevetted captain in 1864, major in 1865, and on the same day lieutenant-colonel, U. S. Volunteers, "for gallant and meritorious service." He participated with his regiment at the Battle of Gettysburg, on Culp's Hill on the right.

He was a member of the Memorial Association which had charge of the battlefield before the appointment of the Commission, and in July, 1893, when the Gettysburg National Park Commission was appointed by Secretary of War Lamont, he became chairman.

While much had been done by the Memorial Association in the laying out of avenues and the placing of regimental monuments, it remained for Colonel Nicholson to re-establish the lines of battle and perfect a system of permanent roads and memorials which make the battlefield the best marked in the world. He received highest commendation from the succeeding Secretaries of War.

Colonel Nicholson was for thirty-seven years recorder-in-chief of the Military Order of the Loyal Legion. At the time of his death he was President of the Valley Forge Commission, and Trustee and Vice-President of the Soldiers' and Sailors' Home at Erie, Pa. He was the author and editor of many publications on the Civil War, and the translator of the History of the Civil War by the Count of Paris. His private library, the largest and best collection of Civil War literature, is now part of the Huntingdon Library at San Marino, Calif. The Loyal Legion erected on Hancock Avenue a monument to his memory. (See illustration facing page 113).

Looking from Culp's Hill, and showing Gettysburg's fine trees.
In the distance is the Phillipoteaux Cyclorama, with its vivid
representation of Pickett's Charge

Jennie Wade House. Here Jennie Wade was killed while
baking bread. The house is practically unchanged; bullet-marks
and other damages have been preserved

Col. John B. Nicholson
Chairman Battlefield Commission

Col. John B. Bachelder
Battlefield Historian

Ricketts' Battery. Ricketts' Battery on East Cemetery Hill
was remanned four times. Owing to the slope, the guns could
not be sufficiently depressed, and the defenders fought with
sticks and stones

CHAPTER IX

THE ARTILLERY

BOTH armies engaged in the Battle of Gettysburg were represented by the three arms of the service, artillery, cavalry, and infantry, and all were engaged at different periods of the three-days' struggle.

The reader of the following account of the artillery is referred to the description of the battle-lines as given in the foregoing account of the battle.

In the organization of the Union Army an ALLOTMENT OF GUNS IN THE UNION ARMY artillery brigade was attached to each corps as follows: 1st Corps—5 batteries, 28 guns; 2nd—5 batteries, 24 guns; 3rd—5 batteries, 30 guns; 5th—5 batteries, 26 guns; 6th—8 batteries, 48 guns; 11th—5 batteries, 26 guns; 12th—4 batteries, 20 guns. In the Cavalry Corps there were 2 brigades of 9 batteries and 50 guns. In addition there was an artillery reserve consisting of 5 brigades and 110 guns, the latter to be sent as supports to the corps artillery when needed. The total number at Gettysburg was 354.

The Chief of Artillery was Brigadier-General Henry J. Hunt. The artillery reserve was in command of Brigadier-General Robert O. Tyler and Captain James M. Robertson.

The commanders of the artillery brigades attached to the different corps of the Union Army were: 1st Corps, Colonel Charles S. Wainwright; 2nd, Captain John G. Hazard; 3rd, Captain George E. Randolph; 5th, Captain Augustus P. Martin; 6th, Colonel Charles H. Tompkins; 11th, Major Thomas W. Osborn; 12th, Lieutenant Edward D. Muhlenburg. The artillery attached to the cavalry was designated Horse Artillery and was commanded by Captains James M. Robertson and John C. Tidball.

ALLOT-
MENT OF
GUNS IN
THE CON-
FEDERATE
ARMY

In the Confederate Army the allotment of artillery was as follows: 1st Corps (Longstreet's) —5 battalions, 84 guns; 2nd (Ewell's)—5 battalions, 84 guns; 3rd (Hill's)—5 battalions, 84 guns; and to the Cavalry Division (Stuart's) —1 battalion and 24 guns. The battalions allotted to the several corps were subdivided. One battalion was assigned to each division of a corps, with 2 battalions in reserve to each corps. As there were 3 corps, each with 3 divisions, it will be readily understood how the 15 battalions above mentioned were allotted. The total number of guns was 272.

The Chief of Artillery was Brigadier-General William N. Pendleton. The commanders of the battalions of the 1st Corps Divisions were: McLaws' Division, Colonel H. C. Cabell; Pickett's Division, Major James Dearing; Hood's Division, Major M. W. Henry; and Reserve

Artillery, Colonel E. P. Alexander and Major B. F. Eshleman. The commanders of the 2nd Corps Divisions were: Early's Division, Lieutenant-Colonel H. P. Jones; Johnson's Division, Major J. W. Latimer; Rodes' Division, Lieutenant-Colonel Thomas H. Carter; Reserve Artillery, Captain Willis J. Dance and Lieutenant-Colonel William Nelson. The battalions of the 3rd Corps were: Anderson's Division, Major John Lane; Heth's Division, Lieutenant-Colonel John J. Garnett; Pender's Division, Major William T. Poague; Reserve Artillery, Majors D. G. McIntosh and W. J. Pegram. The Horse Artillery attached to Stuart's Cavalry Division was commanded by Major R. F. Beckham.

"Brigades" and "battalions" were respectively the Union and Confederate terms for the same formation.

Radical changes have been made in the material of light artillery since 1863. The muzzle-loading guns of that period are obsolete and have been replaced by the modern breech-loading gun of rapid fire and long range. TYPE OF GUNS

The 12-pounder Napoleon was a very popular gun and more were used in the battle than of any other type. It was made of bronze, had a smooth bore and was muzzle-loading. Its round, solid shot weighed 12 pounds. The shrapnel, or spherical case, was a thin shell filled with musket

balls; a bursting charge weighed, with its sabot, 12¼ pounds. The canister, which was a tin can of the diameter of the bore and 6 inches long, filled with cast-iron shot about an inch in diameter, weighed 14 pounds. The sabot, a piece of wood turned to fit the bore, was placed between the powder and the shell, instead of the wads formerly used. It was used only in smoothbore guns that fired conical shells. The Napoleon with its carriage weighed 2,600 pounds, a pretty solid load to be dragged by six powerful horses over ditches, plowed fields, stone walls, and clearings full of stumps and logs. It was a thrilling sight to see a battery brought into action.

Two Whitworth guns attached to Hill's Corps were the only breech-loaders in the battle. There are four now in position on the field, thus placed to show their two positions during the battle. They had a range of nearly 5 miles, and from their position on Oak Ridge on the third day could reach the Round Tops. They used an elongated, 12-pound shell of peculiar shape, cast to follow the rifling. Its whining report could be heard above all others. On account of the blockade only a few Whitworths were imported.

Other types were 10- and 20-pounder Parrotts, 3-inch rifles, a few James guns, and a number of 12- and 24-pounder Howitzers. The 3-inch rifles were favorites with both armies. They used a long shell, and, like the Napoleons and

the Parrotts, had a range of 1½ to 2 miles. The Howitzers were used for dropping shells into the lines of the enemy and not for direct fire.

In the Union Army, 6 guns were usually assigned to a battery; these were divided into a right, middle, and left section. In the Confederate Army, 4 guns were usually used. By a strange coincidence, both armies had 68 batteries at Gettysburg. We can mention only those that deserve special notice on account of service at points of close contact with the enemy. The artillery in both armies was an important factor, more guns being used than at any other battle of the Civil War up to that time. Not only on the main field, but also on the right on East Cavalry Field the artillery played a large part.

NUMBER OF GUNS TO A BATTERY

THE CANNON ON THE FIRST DAY

Marye's Virginia Battery had the distinction of firing the first cannon-shot from its position on Herr Ridge. The first shot in reply was fired by Lieutenant Roder, of Calef's Union Battery attached to the Horse Artillery of Buford's Division of Cavalry. The battery was posted across the Chambersburg or Cashtown road near the position of the statue later erected to the memory of General Reynolds. The other Union batteries engaged on this part of the field were Stevens' 5th Maine, Hall's 2nd Maine, Stewart's,

Reynolds', and Cooper's. The Confederate batteries engaged were Pegram's Battalion and McIntosh's, Garnett's, and Carter's. On the Union 11th Corps line, the batteries of Dilger, Wheeler, and Wilkeson were engaged; the latter on Barlow's Knoll.

The left of the Confederate artillery line on the first day was held by Jones' Battalion of Ewell's Corps, posted south of the Harrisburg road to the right of Barlow's Knoll, where Wilkeson put up a determined resistance. Observing his activity, General Gordon directed Jones to train a section of his guns against him, saying:

> "I can't carry that hill until we get rid of that battery."

Soon Wilkeson fell mortally wounded. To help cover the Union retreat, Heckman's Battery was sent from Cemetery Hill to Carlisle Street, near where the new Academy building now stands. After the retreat of the 11th Corps, the 1st Corps, attacked in front and both flanks, was also compelled to fall back to Cemetery Hill. The batteries on the left of the Union line held their positions at the Seminary building and the railroad cut until almost surrounded, but eventually succeeded in reaching Cemetery Hill with the loss of but one gun from Reynolds' Battery. Heckman in his retreat on Carlisle Street lost two guns.

THE SECOND DAY'S WORK

The batteries on the Emmitsburg road from right to left were Turnbull's, Seely's, and Randolph's. From right to left at the Peach Orchard to Devil's Den were Ames', Clark's, Thompson's, Bigelow's, and Phillips'. Winslow was posted on the Wheatfield and Smith at Devil's Den. At this time Little Round Top, the most vital point for the Union line to hold, was as yet unoccupied by Union troops except as a signal station. General Warren, who arrived on the crest some time after the assault on the Union left began, ordered Hazlett's Battery to be hurried thither. On account of the boulders and trees, horses were of little use and some of the guns were lifted over the rocks bodily. Infantry troops were also hurried up by the foresight of Warren, and the position was held. *UNION ARTILLERY LINE*

Beginning on the right of the Union line, some of the 12th Corps guns were posted on Power's Hill, with one section on Culp's Hill and others in reserve. Between Culp's Hill and the Baltimore Pike, on what is now called Stevens' Knoll, an important position was held by Stevens' 5th Maine Battery. When the Union forces were falling back to a new position on Cemetery Hill, General Hancock ordered Stevens, who had already distinguished himself, to

"Take your battery on that hill and stop the enemy from coming up that ravine."

Stevens obeyed and the advance of the Confederate forces was checked.

On East Cemetery Hill, Weidrich, Ricketts, Cooper, Reynolds, and Stewart held the artillery line, with Taft in the rear on the Baltimore Pike and Cemetery Hill. Huntingdon held the crest of Cemetery Hill to the left, where the line was continued at Ziegler's Grove by the batteries of the 2nd Corps. From right to left they were posted in the following order: Woodruff, Arnold, Cushing, Brown, and Rorty, and on the left, Rorty, Thomas, Dow, and Watson. Some withdrawals and some additions were made during the progress of the battle.

CONFEDER-
ATE ARTIL-
LERY LINE
The Confederate artillery battalions were posted right to left on Seminary Ridge in the following order: Henry, Cabell, Alexander, Eshleman, Dearing, Poague, Lane, Pegram, Garnett, McIntosh, and Dance. Carter was posted north of the town in the vicinity of the railroad cut. Nelson and Latimer were on the east on Benner's Hill, the latter occupying the extreme left of the Confederate line. Jones' Battalion was in reserve.

LEE'S
ASSAULT
General Lee's assault on Meade's line was to be progressive from right to left. When Longstreet began on the right, Ewell on the left was expected to make a demonstration against the Union right. Contrary to Lee's plan, Ewell's attack, other than some artillery firing, was delayed until the battle on the left had ended.

The battle on the left was begun by the artillery. At about 3 o'clock the Union batteries at the Peach Orchard opened against the Confederate line on Seminary Ridge. A total of 46 Confederate guns were operated in return. After an artillery engagement of about half an hour, Hood's infantry moved against the Union left. They were followed by McLaws and later by the brigades of Hill's Corps. These, from right to left, were Perry, Wilcox, and Wright. The attack ended with the attack of Wright at sunset. Fifty-five guns on Hill's line were brought into action as the battle progressed from right to left.

During this attack on the Union left, the artillery fire on both lines was kept up for more than two hours without intermission, and the losses were heavy both in men and guns. Colonel E. P. Alexander says:

"Fickling's Battery of four 12-pounder Howitzers had two of them dismounted and forty cannoneers killed or wounded."

On Little Round Top, Weed, in command of the infantry, was fatally wounded. Hazlett, in command of the battery, leaned over him to catch his dying words and fell dead on his body, pierced by a sharp-shooter's bullet from Devil's Den. Lieutenant Rittenhouse succeeded Hazlett in command. In addition to the loss of Hazlett, there was a loss of 12 men of the battery.

Other Union batteries rendered very efficient service after Sickles' advance line had been crushed and his forces obliged to retire and abandon many of their guns. This was a critical moment—unless a line of guns could be posted in the gap, the Confederates had a fair chance of getting through to the Taneytown road. In this emergency, Bigelow's Battery, after its withdrawal from its first position on the Wheatfield road, was posted, by McGilvery's order, at the Trostle buildings and ordered to hold that position at all hazards until a line of guns could be hurried up to fill the vacant space. Holding his position until 40 guns were brought from the advance line and other parts of the field, Bigelow lost 28 men and upwards of 80 horses. He was obliged to abandon 4 of his guns; 2 were withdrawn by hand. Somewhat to the rear of Bigelow, Watson's Battery also gave a good account of itself. At Devil's Den, Smith's Battery had put up a good fight until they were surrounded. Four of Smith's guns were posted on the hill back of the Den, while 2 were on the left on the edge of the ridge. Smith was finally obliged to withdraw, leaving 3 of his guns in the hands of the enemy. The guns to the left were saved. Thompson's Battery lost 1 gun on its withdrawal from near the Peach Orchard. After Meade had rectified his line and brought up additional supports, a counter-attack was made

and the battle on the left ended, the Confederates gaining some advantage in the vicinity of Big Round Top and Devil's Den. All the Union guns, with the exception of those of Smith and Thompson, were recaptured.

The attack on the Union right consisted of three separate engagements. First in order was the artillery duel between the Union batteries on Cemetery Hill and the Confederate batteries on Benner's Hill, east of Rock Creek. There Nelson's Battalion on Benner's Hill, north of the Hanover road, and Latimer's Battalion to the south were in an exposed position. The engagement did not begin until the attack on the left was well advanced and was of short duration, but nowhere on the field of Gettysburg was such havoc wrought by artillery on artillery as that on Latimer's Battalion in the loss of men, guns, and horses in such a short space of time. Major Latimer, who was but twenty years old, had distinguished himself as an expert in this branch of the service, and was known in the army as "the Boy Major." He was mortally wounded and died a few days after the battle. Two officers and eight men were killed, and two officers and thirty-five men wounded. Thirty horses were killed, and almost all the sixteen guns were wrecked or destroyed. There were some slight losses among the Union guns. These were protected by lunettes which have been preserved.

ATTACK ON CEMETERY HILL

The second and third engagements were the attack of Johnson's Division on Culp's Hill, and a little later Early's attack on Cemetery Hill. Both took place when the battle on the left was about over. Johnson's attack was principally confined to the infantry.

Early's attack on Cemetery Hill began at sunset and continued until 9 o'clock. The fight among the Union guns was a hand-to-hand struggle in which stones, clubs, side-arms, and clubbed muskets were used. On account of the sharp incline of Cemetery Hill to the east where the advance of Hays and Hoke was made, the guns on the top of the hill could not be depressed enough to be effective. Stevens, farther south on the knoll, however, was in a position to enfilade the assaulting column from right to left, and caused great losses in the line of assault before it reached the Union guns on the crest. The hill was soon shrouded in darkness and it was difficult to tell friend from foe.

At this critical time, Carroll's Brigade of the 2nd Corps, sent by General Hancock, arrived at a double-quick and succeeded in driving the assailants down the hill.

THE THIRD DAY'S ARTILLERY DUEL

On the morning of the 3rd there was another battle at Culp's Hill. At 4 o'clock the Union

batteries on Power's Hill, with others posted on the Baltimore Pike, opened a terrific artillery attack on Johnson, who was in possession of the Union works in the vicinity of Spangler's Spring. These had been vacated on the afternoon of the 2nd by troops sent to the left to assist in repelling Longstreet's assault. This engagement on the morning of the 3rd continued until 10 o'clock. Johnson was compelled to withdraw and the Union forces regained their vacated line.

From 10 o'clock until 1 there was comparative quiet. Lee's plan was to attack Meade's left center with artillery, to be followed by infantry. Seventy-five guns were advanced from the line of the 2nd Corps and posted from the Peach Orchard on the right north on the plain in front of the Spangler Woods, where they joined the right of a line of 63 guns, a total of 138. The first were in command of Colonel E. P. Alexander and the latter in charge of Colonel E. L. Walker.

The Union artillery line had been strengthened by bringing up additional batteries in support in the rear. The number of Union guns that could be brought to bear against the Confederate line was only about 85.

At 1 o'clock two guns of Miller's Battery of the Washington Artillery of New Orleans, posted near the Peach Orchard, fired two shots in rapid succession as a signal for the Confederate artillery. Instantly the Union guns replied and the

air was filled with screaming, whistling shot and shell. An occasional Whitworth missile, from Oak Hill on the north, could be heard above the din of all the others. The batteries on the Union line, especially at The Angle, were badly damaged. Others were at once brought up with additional supplies of ammunition. While the losses among the gunners in men and horses were heavy, the losses inflicted upon the infantry were comparatively light, on account of the protection afforded by the stone wall and the undulations of the ground.

After the duel had been in operation for about an hour and a half, Meade and Hunt ordered the Union artillery to stop firing in order to cool the guns, save ammunition, and allow the atmosphere to clear of the dense cloud of smoke that enshrouded the field from line to line. The cessation of firing led the Confederates to believe that the Union line had been destroyed and that the opportune time had come for the advance of the infantry, and it was therefore ordered to proceed.

After the Confederate column, 15,000 in number and a mile long, had moved out to the rising ground in front of the Spangler Woods, the Union artillery, from Cemetery Hill on the right to Little Round Top on the left, opened along the whole line, and continued without intermission until part of the assaulting forces had crossed the stone wall at The Angle where

the struggle was hand-to-hand, and where double grape and canister were used at 10 yards. The Confederates were subjected to an artillery fire on both flanks and front, but with cannon to the right, cannon to the left, and cannon in front, the advance continued until its culmination at The Angle, where the Battle of Gettysburg ended with this, the greatest artillery duel the world had known.

The artillery was not the only factor in repulsing the Confederate charge; after the lines were within range of the musketry fire the infantry played the more important part. During the retreat of the assaulting column, artillery fire was resumed on both sides, and was continued until the survivors of the assaulting column had reached their original line on Seminary Ridge.

Meanwhile, out to the east, on the Rummel Farm, the Confederate Cavalry in command of Stuart began a movement to reach the rear of Meade's line. This movement was frustrated by the Union Cavalry in command of Gregg and Custer. In this cavalry fight artillery was used by both armies.

While all the Union batteries rendered efficient service, two at The Angle deserve special mention. Cushing, to the right of the copse of trees, with one of his guns at the wall, said to Webb,

"I will give them one more shot."

He fell dead just before the Confederate Armistead crossed the wall and was mortally wounded.

Cowan's Battery, in place of Brown's that had been withdrawn, had 5 guns on the left of the clump of trees and 1 on the right near Cushing's. It fired double grape and canister when the Confederates were within 10 yards of the guns, literally blowing the men to pieces. Cushing's Battery had the distinction of sustaining the heaviest loss of all batteries engaged in the battle.

CONCLU-
SION

The loss in the Union Artillery was 113 killed, 592 wounded, 54 missing, a total of 769.

The Confederate loss was 94 killed, 438 wounded, 77 missing, a total of 608.

When it is remembered that the complement of men for a Union 6-gun battery was usually about 100, and that of a Confederate 4-gun battery proportionately less, it will be seen that the percentage of loss in the artillery was well up to that of the other arms of the service. It should also be kept in mind that not all the batteries were engaged, both sides holding reserves.

> *"On this field the cause of Liberty and Union gained a positive and permanent triumph. When Lee marched out of Pennsylvania it was already determined that the American Union was indissoluble.*
> —JOSEPH B. FORAKER, 1887.

North Carolina Monument. Gutzon Borglum, Sculptor

Culp's Hill. Here the Union troops held their line late in the afternoon of the Second Day

Col. Emmor B. Cope
Topographic Engineer of Battlefield

The Rostrum in the Cemetery. From the vine-draped Rostrum many famous speakers have addressed the throngs that visit Gettysburg on Memorial Day. (See page 158)

CHAPTER X

GETTYSBURG AND ITS MILITARY PARK

THE Gettysburg National Military Park lies entirely within the limits of Adams County, Pennsylvania. Gettysburg, the county-seat, is situated about 8 miles from the Mason and Dixon's line, the southern boundary of the State. It was founded in 1780, and named for its founder, James Gettys.

At the time of the battle the town had a population of about 2,000. Little did the quiet inhabitants expect that its peaceful environs—Oak Hill, Seminary Ridge, Culp's Hill, Cemetery Hill, the Round Tops, and Devil's Den—would witness the most sanguinary struggle of the Civil War, and that Gettysburg would gain a lasting fame, unequaled by the most noted battlefields of the Old World. Not even the commanders, Meade and Lee, knew where they would meet in battle array. Like two giant storm-clouds, the two armies neared each other for days, neither foreseeing where they would mingle their lightnings in the storm of battle. Advance forces met and clashed while making reconnaissances—and Gettysburg and its vicinity was selected by accident rather than by design.

What fame Gettysburg enjoyed was due chiefly to its College, then called Pennsylvania, now Gettysburg, and to its Lutheran Theological Seminary. The town had been the home for some years of Thaddeus Stevens, the "Great Commoner," life-long champion of human rights, author of the free school system of Pennsylvania, and after his removal to Lancaster, in 1842, a brilliant leader in the House of Representatives during the war. The vicinity furnished its full quota of soldiers, though none

of its companies except one, Company K, First Pennsylvania Reserves, participated in the battle, the rest being on duty elsewhere.

The population of Gettysburg has increased to 5,500. The College and Seminary are still flourishing. The College has an enrollment of over 600 students. A Reserve Officers Training Corps has been added to the course, and students are being instructed in military tactics by United States Army officers.

The area of Gettysburg National Military Park, including East Cavalry Field 3 miles east of the town, and South Cavalry Field 3 miles south, is nearly 40 square miles. The part surrounding Gettysburg covers about 24 square miles, and was the scene of the principal engagements on July 1st, 2nd, and 3rd, 1863. The Government owns a total of 2,532 acres; the remainder is held by private owners.

The first organization in charge of the battlefield was the Gettysburg Battlefield Memorial Association, upon which the Legislature of Pennsylvania, on April 30th, 1864, conferred the rights of a corporation. In 1867–68 the Legislature appropriated $6,000 to be applied to the purchase of portions of the battle-grounds and the general purposes for which the Association was incorporated. The money was used to secure the portion of Culp's Hill upon which the breastworks were still standing; the section of East Cemetery Hill where Stewart's, Reynolds', Ricketts', Cooper's and Weidrich's batteries were posted, where the lunettes still remain; and also a small piece of ground on the slope and summit of Little Round Top. This purchase was the nucleus of what became, by additional purchases of the Association and later of the Gettysburg National Park Commission, the present Gettysburg National Military Park.

The Legislatures of the Northern States represented in

the battle contributed various sums for the prosecution of the work, and from time to time new members of the Association were appointed. As the appropriations were received, additional land was acquired and avenues were laid out. The erection of monuments to the different regiments was begun by the State of Massachusetts in 1879. In 1894, the whole property, about 600 acres of land, with 17 miles of avenues, giving access to 320 monuments, was transferred to the United States Government. The Gettysburg National Military Park was established by Act of Congress, approved February 11th, 1895, and the Secretary of War appointed the Gettysburg National Park Commission: Colonel John P. Nicholson, Pennsylvania, Chairman, John B. Bachelder, Massachusetts, and Brigadier-General William H. Forney, Alabama. Colonel E. B. Cope was selected as topographical engineer.

Upon the death of General Forney, Major William M. Robbins, of North Carolina, was appointed to fill the vacancy. John B. Bachelder was succeeded by Major Charles A. Richardson, of New York. On the death of Major Robbins, General L. L. Lomax, of Virginia, was appointed. General Lomax died May 28th, 1913, and Major Richardson on January 24th, 1917. Colonel Nicholson, the last surviving member of the Commission, died on March 8th, 1922. All Commissioners, with the exception of John B. Bachelder, served in the Battle of Gettysburg, and he reached the field immediately after the battle, continuing his interest and his historical researches until his death. On the death of Colonel Nicholson, Colonel E. B. Cope was appointed Superintendent.

The Park is a monument to the devotion of this Commission, which was in active operation for thirty years. The present superintendent (1932) is Colonel E. E. Davis, a native of Iowa, commissioned Major Quartermaster

Reserve Corps, March 6th, 1917, who served overseas in the World War.

The development begun by the Association included laying out of avenues and erecting of regimental monuments, but nothing was done toward converting the avenues into permanent roads. The different lines of battle were not accurately marked, and important sections of land remained in private hands. By the end of the year the new Commission had made preliminary survey of 20 miles of avenues and proposed avenues, and, the following year, began construction. Gradually the whole field was made accessible by almost 35 miles of telford and macadam avenues. These avenues, as their names indicate, show the important positions occupied by the contending forces. Stone bridges were built across the streams. Miles of pipe-fencing and post-and-rail fencing were constructed, the former along the avenues indicating the battle-lines and the latter to enclose the Government land. Five steel observation towers were erected on prominent points, affording views in all directions.

An important task of the Commission was the accurate marking of the lines of battle of the opposing forces. Prominent commanders of both armies visited the field and assisted in locating the positions of the corps, divisions, and brigades. Suitable monuments and markers were then erected, upon which were placed bronze tablets with inscriptions giving an account of the operations of each corps, division, and brigade.

Suitable markers show the locations of the headquarters of the Commander-in-Chief, as well as of the corps commanders of both armies. Six equestrian statues have been erected by States; also, imposing State monuments by New York, Pennsylvania, Virginia, and North Carolina. There are many smaller markers, placed by States and other organizations. Bronze statues of division and

brigade commanders have been erected. There are a number of National Monuments; one in the National Cemetery, placed where Lincoln stood when making his immortal address at the dedication of the cemetery, November 19th, 1863; also one in the south end of the cemetery bearing a bust of Lincoln, and another on Hancock Avenue in memory of the troops belonging to the Regular Army. All the positions held by the Regulars have been marked. The total number of monuments to date is 845. Four hundred and fifteen guns indicate the positions of the artillery brigades and battalions.

The relief maps of the Gettysburg National Military Park, on exhibition at the office in the Federal Building, in Gettysburg, were designed by the Engineer of the Commission, Colonel E. B. Cope, and built under his supervision. The largest reproduces 24 square miles and gives a correct delineation of all the topographical features of the Park. Many of the monuments and markers erected by the Commission were also designed by Colonel Cope. The imposing stone gateway at the entrance to Hancock Avenue was proposed by the Chairman, Colonel Nicholson, and designed by the Engineer. This gateway is built of native granite taken from the battlefield.

Celebrations, reunions, dedications, and campfires almost without number have been held at Gettysburg, bringing to the field those who participated in the battle, their families and friends, and many other visitors. For many years, until a permanent camp was established at Mt. Gretna, the National Guard of Pennsylvania encamped on the field. The two greatest occasions were the Twenty-fifth Anniversary in 1888, and the Fiftieth Anniversary in 1913. The latter was attended by almost 55,000 survivors of the two armies. Ample accommodations were provided for their comfort and enjoyment. The time extended over a period of eight days, June 29th to

July 6th, and every State in the Union was represented. The men who had met as mortal enemies fifty years before now met as brothers. The American soldier is not only a good fighter but also a good friend. Many donned their uniforms of '63, some of Blue and some of Gray, but in the wearers great changes had been wrought. The sturdy veterans who in the vigor of their youth met fifty years before in battle, returned grizzled with age and the ravages of war, many bearing scars. With keen interest, in pairs and groups, they moved from place to place relating to each other their experiences. In startling contrast to the 45,000 casualties of '63 there were only seven deaths, and these from the infirmities of age and natural causes. The President of the United States and many able speakers from all sections of the country made addresses to large audiences. It was an event never to be forgotten and did much finally to heal the animosities engendered by the war.

On July 3, 1922, Marines from Quantico, Va., under the command of Brigadier-General Smedley D. Butler, repeated Pickett's Charge as it was made in 1863, and on July 4th conducted it as such a charge would be made under present warfare conditions with modern equipment and maneuvers. President Harding, General Pershing, and many others prominent in the State and Nation enjoyed the display.

For many years the West Point Military Academy seniors visited the field, usually in the month of May, remaining several days in order to study the strategical and tactical features of the battle in preparation for a required thesis. These visits have been discontinued since the World War.

In May, 1917, a training-camp for World War soldiers was established within the limits of the Park. The 4th, 7th and 58th Regiments of U. S. Infantry were transferred

from El Paso, Texas, augmented by recruits, and divided into six United States Regular Regiments, viz.: 4th, 7th, 58th, 59th, 60th, and 61st. After being trained they were sent either to other camps or to the battlefields of France. During the year 1918 a unit of Tank Service was trained on the battlefield.

The fortifications remaining within the park include a line of earthworks on Culp's Hill, which was thrown up by the Union troops of the 12th Corps. On East Cemetery Hill there are a number of lunettes at the position held by the Union batteries. The stone wall along the west side of Hancock Avenue, extending from the Taneytown Road to some distance south of the Angle, where Armistead crossed it in Pickett's Charge, is well preserved, and practically the same as at the time of the battle. There are some stone walls on the south side of Little Round Top that were erected and used by the Union forces. At the base of Big Round Top and along Seminary Ridge are long stone walls, erected and used by the Confederates. The boulders in the vicinity of Devil's Den and the Round Tops afforded natural defenses for both armies. A line of earthworks on South Hancock Avenue is still in good condition.

The physical features of the Park are both varied and interesting. Standing in bold relief in the background at a distance of about 8 miles is a continuation of the Blue Ridge, designated locally as the South Mountain. This range, bounding the Shenandoah Valley of Virginia and the Cumberland Valley of Pennsylvania, screened the advance of the Confederate Army, and it was at the Cashtown Gap that General Lee ordered a concentration of his forces before his advance on Gettysburg.

The entire surface of the Park consists of low ridges and intervening valleys, beginning on the north in Herr's Ridge, upon which Heth's Division was deployed at the

opening of the battle on July 1st. Opposite this ridge, and extending in the same direction, is McPherson Ridge, where the Union cavalry forces under Buford were deployed. Along Willoughby Run, which flows between these ridges, the battle opened on July 1, 1863. The next elevation, immediately north and west of the town, is known as Oak Ridge at its northern extremity and as far south as the Chambersburg Pike; from this point to its southern extremity it is called Seminary Ridge, taking its name from the yet existing Lutheran Theological Seminary. It was held by the Union Army on the first day of the battle and formed its principal line of defense. On the second and third days it was the principal Confederate line.

Seminary Ridge at its southern extremity drops off to a small ravine beyond which is Warfield Ridge, which extends in a southerly direction opposite Big Round Top; this formed the right of the Confederate line of battle on the second and third days.

South and southwest of the town is Cemetery Ridge, of which Big Round Top and Little Round Top are spurs, named from the Evergreen Cemetery and the site of the National Cemetery after the battle.

Cemetery Ridge formed the main line of battle of the Union Army during the battles of the 2nd and 3rd. A short distance east of the cemetery it bends sharply to the right, forming two rocky and wooded prominences, Culp's Hill and Spangler's Hill. Between Seminary Ridge on the west and Cemetery Ridge on the east, a low ridge along the line of the Emmitsburg Road is designated Emmitsburg Road Ridge. This extends to the Peach Orchard. It was crossed on the afternoon of the 3rd by the assaulting column of Pickett's Charge, and is one of the interesting points of the battle. Another ridge on the west front of Little Round Top contains Devil's Den, a

mass of enormous granite rocks, apparently tossed in confusion by some giant hand. In this picturesque spot
Longstreet made his famous assault against the Union
left on the afternoon of July 2nd. The trend of these
various ridges conforms generally to that of the Blue
Ridge.

There are no large streams on the battlefield. The
largest is Marsh Creek, only a small part of which is
within the Park area. On the east is Rock Creek, extending the whole length of the Park, so named on account of
the immense boulders within the channel and along the
borders. On the north and west of Gettysburg is Willoughby Run, also extending the entire length of the Park and
flowing south to Marsh Creek. Another small stream is
Plum Run, near the center, beginning on the Codori farm
and running south through the gorge at the Round Tops;
this was crossed and recrossed by both armies during the
second and third days. Lying wholly within the Potomac
basin, all the streams flow south.

The highest point within the Park is Big Round Top
on the south, which rises to an elevation of 786 feet, and
is visible for miles in all directions. From Big Round Top,
Little Round Top, Culp's Hill, Cemetery Hill, and Oak
Hill there are extensive panoramic views. Aside from the
historic association there is much in the magnificent and
beautiful scenery to interest the visitor. In the woods
and meadows, in the glens and vales of the battlefield
there are romantic and charming bits of landscape. The
prospect from the National Cemetery as the sun disap-
pears behind the South Mountain is one of great beauty
and impressiveness.

A large portion of the Park is covered with timber,
chiefly the different varieties of oak, hickory, ash, poplar,
elm, gum, cedar, and pine. Many of the groves are forests
primeval, and in the fall the lofty pines of Big Round Top,

contrasting with the crimson of the gigantic oaks covering it from base to summit and the gray-lichened surface of the massive boulders, form a striking and beautiful picture. Much care is given to the protection of the groves, in order to preserve the original condition of the field. Tree-surgery has prolonged the lives of trees of special historic interest. Visitors return year after year in spring to see the glorious masses of dogwood and redbud.

East Cavalry Field, 3 miles east of Gettysburg, is the point from which Stuart's Cavalry started to move round the right wing of the Union Army in order to reach the rear of Meade's line at the time of Pickett's Charge. South Cavalry Field, 3 miles south of Gettysburg, was held by Farnsworth's Brigade of Kilpatrick's Division, and Merritt's Brigade of Buford's Division. All these positions have been marked with suitable tablets. The Cavalry Fields, though not contiguous to the main field, are important parts of the National Military Park.

Two railroads and ten concrete or macadam roads radiating from the town like the spokes of a wheel, provide ample approaches. The Lincoln Highway, entering via the Chambersburg Pike and continuing on the York Pike, gives a through route from west to east, and the Harrisburg Road leads directly to the State Capital. The Emmitsburg Road runs southwest to Emmitsburg, and thence to Frederick and Washington. The Baltimore Pike is a through route to Baltimore and the South. The Hanover Road runs to Hanover on the east. There are also the Taneytown and Hagerstown roads, the latter the line of General Lee's retreat.

A uniformed guide service with an established schedule of rates was authorized by the Secretary of War in 1916. There are interesting collections of Civil War relics at the Jennie Wade House, the Lee Museum, and other places. A single year has brought 800,000 visitors to the field. The average yearly number is 700,000.

CHAPTER XI

THE SIGNAL CORPS

THE wig-wag system of signaling was invented by Assistant Surgeon A. J. Myer in 1859. His first pupil was Colonel E. P. Alexander, who four years later commanded Longstreet's Artillery on the afternoon of July 3, at Gettysburg. In his "Military Memoirs" Colonel Alexander says:

> "In October, 1859, I was assigned to special duty with Assistant Surgeon A. J. Myer to experiment with a system of military signals which had been devised and offered to the War Department. It was based upon the use of Baine's telegraphic alphabet, which formed the letters by the use of only two elements, the dot and the dash. The Morse alphabet uses four—dot, short dash, long dash and interval between dashes. By waving the flag to the left for a dot, and to the right for a dash, any letter could be indicated by a few waves."

Colonel Alexander was the Signal Officer of the Confederates at Bull Run. Subsequently the Signal Corps was an important branch of the service in all the armies of North and South. In every important campaign and on every bloody battlefield, the white flags with a red center dispatched important messages, carried warnings of impending danger, and announcements of victory or defeat.

When a campaign was in progress, the position of a Signal Officer, usually in advance of the Army, was one of great danger. Stations were established from which observations could be made of the movements of the enemy and from which messages could be sent back. The casualties during the Civil War in the Signal Corps showed more killed than wounded.

When the Army of the Potomac began its movement in the Gettysburg campaign, two Signal Officers were appointed to each corps, with Captain Lemuel B. Norton as Chief. Captain Norton gives a very complete report of his services during the campaign.

Arriving with General Buford on June 30th, a Signal Officer took position in the cupola of the College building and reported to Buford the whereabouts of the enemy. Captain Norton says:

"On July 1st, general headquarters remained at Taneytown. A station of observation was established first on the college and subsequently on the courthouse in Gettysburg, and reports of the positions, numbers and movements of the enemy sent by signals to General Howard, on Cemetery Hill. Two reconnaissances were made from Gettysburg on the afternoon of this day, for the information of General Hancock, by the Signal Officer attached to his staff.

"Late in the evening of this day I was directed by the Chief-of-Staff to start at daylight the next morning with the Signal Officers in reserve and rejoin the commanding general on the field of Gettysburg. Before

11 A.M., on July 2nd, every desirable point of observation was occupied by a Signal Officer, and communication opened from General Meade's headquarters to those of every corps commander.

"Additional stations were established at Howard's headquarters, Stevens' Knoll, Little Round Top, and one for a short time for the cavalry on the Hanover road two and a half miles east of the town."

On the afternoon of the second day, when General Lee was forming his line of assault on Meade's left, the signal station in full view on Little Round Top gave the Confederates much concern, and McLaws' Division made a detour to the Black Horse Tavern in order to avoid observation.

Colonel Alexander says:

"That wretched little signal station upon Round Top that day caused one of our divisions to lose over two hours, and probably delayed our assault nearly that long. During that time a Federal corps arrived near Round Top and became an important factor in the action which followed."

When General Warren, Chief Engineer of the Army of the Potomac, reached Little Round Top on the afternoon of the second day, he found there only the Signal Officers. He observed that this was the key of the whole position, and that the Union troops in the woods in front could not see the ground before them, so that the enemy could come upon them unawares. He ordered that a shot be fired by Smith's Battery, posted

on the hill back of Devil's Den, into the woods in front. At once a commotion in the line of the advancing Confederates caused their muskets to gleam in the sunlight.

He says:

> "This motion revealed to me the enemy's line of battle already formed and far outflanking our troops. The discovery was intensely thrilling and almost appalling. I immediately sent a written dispatch to General Meade to send a division at least to me.
>
> "While I was still alone with the Signal Officer, the musket-balls began to fly around us, and he was about to fold his flags and withdraw, but remained, at my request, and kept waving in defiance."

The Signal Officer and his men were exposed to the artillery fire and the deadly bullets of the Confederate sharp-shooters secreted among the boulders at Devil's Den. Seven men were killed or seriously wounded. At a most critical phase, Captain Hall signaled to Meade's headquarters,

> "A heavy column of the enemy's infantry, about ten thousand, is moving from opposite our extreme left toward our right."

On the afternoon of the 3rd, the signals told General Hunt when the Confederates were forming their lines for Pickett's Charge:

> "They are moving out to make a charge."

The signal station was at Meade's headquarters, which on the afternoon of the 3rd, because of the Confederate artillery fire from Semi-

nary Ridge, were moved to Power's Hill, where Slocum's headquarters were located.

The Signal Officer in charge at Meade's headquarters was Captain D. E. Castle. Captain Norton in his report says:

> "On July 3rd, when the enemy made their furious attack upon our center at Gettysburg, Captain Castle occupied a signal station at General Meade's headquarters, near Cemetery Hill, and remained there on duty after all others had been driven away. His flagmen had also left with his signal equipment, under the impression that their officer had gone with the rest. Having occasion to send a couple of important messages to the general commanding, then at General Slocum's headquarters, Captain Castle quickly cut a pole, extemporized a signal flag from a bed-sheet procured near-by, and sent his dispatches through."

The signal station on Little Round Top is the only one on the battlefield that has been permanently marked. A bronze plate, attached to the side of the large boulder where the station was located, was placed there by the survivors.

The Confederates established their chief signal station in the cupola of the Seminary building, which commanded an extensive field of operations. From here General Lee got his information about the progress of the battle.

After the withdrawal of the Confederate forces, the Union signal station was re-established on the College, and a message reported to the

general commanding that the enemy had vacated their position and later that they were retreating.

COLONEL JOHN B. BACHELDER

Colonel John B. Bachelder was born at Gilmanton, N. H., in 1825, and died in Nottingham, N. H., in 1894. By order of the United States authorities, he went to Gettysburg soon after the battle and began his collection of facts for a history of the conflict. He served as a director of the Gettysburg Battlefield Memorial Association and a member of the Battlefield Commission, until his death.

Colonel Bachelder is the author of an important "Geometrical Drawing of the Battle," a descriptive key to the painting of Longstreet's Assault, and a complete set of maps showing the positions held by the opposing forces at different periods of the battle. He conceived the idea of the "High Water Mark" monument and tablet, designed it and collected funds for its erection. (See illustration facing page 113).

COLONEL EMMOR BRADLEY COPE

Colonel Emmor Bradley Cope, Topographic Engineer of the Battlefield, was born in Chester County, Pa., in 1834, and died in Gettysburg in 1927. He enlisted in Company A, 1st Pennsylvania Reserves, June 10, 1861, was promoted to Captain on staff of General Warren and served under Warren in the Battle of Gettysburg. He served actively in twenty-six battles of the war. Appointed to service with the Commission in 1893, he devoted the remainder of his life to the development of the battlefield. He designed many of the markers and monuments and constructed various relief maps, the largest showing accurately the topographic features of 24 square miles. Upon the death of Colonel Nicholson he served as superintendent of the field until his death at the age of 92. (See illustration facing page 129).

Center of Union Line, Third Day. The center of the Union line, showing the Angle and the rounded clump of trees toward which Pickett directed his charge. (Arrow indicates high-water mark.)

High-Water Mark. This monument, erected close to the rounded clump of trees toward which Pickett directed his charge, marks the turning-point of the conflict

Memorial to Lincoln. Erected in memory of Lincoln's Address
Henry K. Bush-Brown, Sculptor

CHAPTER XII

THE HOSPITALS

THE Battle of Gettysburg was the most momentous battle of the Civil War, not only in the strategic and national issues involved, but in its fearful destruction of human life. During the three-days' struggle the Union Army sustained a loss of 3,155 killed, 14,529 wounded, and 5,365 captured and missing. The loss of the Confederate Army was 2,592 killed, 12,709 wounded, and 5,150 captured or missing. In all, 5,747 men were killed outright and 27,238 were wounded.

After the withdrawal of the armies, a stupendous task confronted the surgeons—the care of the wounded. On account of the shifting scenes of the battle, some of these could not be removed until the night of the third day, and a few were not reached until the morning of the fourth. The suffering of many under a broiling July sun was intense. Without water, some died of thirst. As soon as possible the litter-bearers carried the living to the rear, where they were loaded in the ambulances and taken to the field hospitals established behind the lines. In addition, a number of public buildings and some private residences were used as hospitals.

HOSPITALS IN GETTYSBURG

On account of the forced retreat of the Union forces on the afternoon of the first day, the Union dead and wounded were left in the hands of the Confederates, and Seminary Ridge, at first a Union stronghold, became for the next two days part of the main line of the Confederates, the peace-time occupants of the campus having fled. From the Seminary building General Lee directed the progress of the battle, and for a longer period than any other public building it was used for a hospital. Immediately after the retreat of the Confederate Army more than 400 Confederate wounded were counted in the building and in tents on the campus. In addition, there were over 200 Union soldiers. Lying side by side, helpless as children, the wounded received for eight weeks the ministrations of surgeons, nurses, agents of the Sanitary and Christian Commissions, Sisters of Charity, Patriotic Daughters of Lancaster, and citizens of Gettysburg.

Among the Confederates were Generals Kemper and Trimble, both of whom had been wounded during Pickett's Charge on the third day. General Trimble had had his leg amputated, and no effort was made to remove him during the retreat. General Kemper started with the retreating army, but his wounds were so serious that he was obliged to stop, and the

pursuing Union forces took him a prisoner and brought him back. Both men were transferred to the Seminary building and given careful surgical treatment. Trimble's audacity often tried the patience of the attendants, and he was eventually sent to Fort Warren, near Boston, and held there as a prisoner for twenty-one months.

A noted Union inmate of the Seminary hospital was Lieutenant-Colonel George F. McFarland, of McAlisterville, Juniata County, Pa. During the first day Colonel McFarland commanded the 151st Pennsylvania Infantry. His regiment, after being greatly depleted, was compelled to withdraw from its position near Reynolds Grove to the neighborhood of the Seminary building, where he was severely wounded by a minie ball that shattered both legs. His right leg was amputated and the other remained permanently crippled. He again narrowly escaped death in the Seminary, as he had been transferred from the room on the northeast corner of the first floor just before a shell entered and shattered the furniture.

As the wounded recovered sufficiently to be moved, they were taken to the cities or to the general hospital established by the Government 1¾ miles east of Gettysburg.

The main building of Pennsylvania College sheltered chiefly Union soldiers who were brought

in from the line of the 11th Corps north of the town. Its large halls and many rooms afforded accommodations for about 400 men. From 4.30 on the afternoon of the first day (Wednesday) until the night of Friday, the town, except part of the southern end, was occupied by the Confederate Army, and facilities for helping the wounded were limited. Food was scarce, and there was suffering not only among the wounded but also among the citizens. Notwithstanding the many dangers and hindrances, a number of brave Gettysburg women did all that was humanly possible to bring relief to the patients at the College.

After the Confederate retreat, conditions improved. Many supplies were sent in by the Government and by the Sanitary and Christian Commissions. Country produce, such as butter, milk, and eggs, was brought in from a distance. The country adjacent to the town could do little or nothing as it had been laid waste by the contending armies. The railroad, destroyed by the Confederates during their movement to York on June 27th, could not be put in order for shipping until July 7th, when it was kept busy carrying away the wounded. Confederates who were held as prisoners of war were either paroled or sent to prison camps as soon as they were able to be moved. Union wounded, when able, were transferred to the general

hospital east of the town, and at the end of July all the College wounded were gone, and the work of cleaning and preparing it for the return of the students for the fall term was begun.

The first church to be used was Christ Lutheran on Chambersburg Street, commonly known as the College Church. Like the Seminary building and the College, it was near the scene of the first day's battle. Both armies were represented there. At St. Francis Xavier Catholic Church, on West High Street, many wounded were tenderly cared for, the greater number from the scene of the second and third days' battles. On Sunday morning after the battle, twelve Sisters of Charity from the convent at Emmitsburg, Md., arrived, bringing with them bandages, sponges, refreshments, and clothing. As they approached they passed over a large part of the battlefield, and horrifying sights prepared them for their work. They directed the nursing in the town hospitals, and the Gettysburg ladies already at work gave the most cheerful obedience, grateful for their skill and experience. Readers should realize that there were none of the modern facilities for nursing, and that antiseptics were yet unknown.

A distinguished Union officer in St. Francis Xavier Church was Colonel H. S. Huidekoper, of Meadville, Pa., who was twice wounded

during the battle of the first day near the McPherson barn. In a letter to Honorable Charles F. McKenna, of Pittsburgh, Pa., he says:

"I reached the Catholic Church on High Street, Gettysburg, on July 1st, 1863, about half-past five in the afternoon, having walked in from the McPherson Barn on the Chambersburg Pike, with my right arm wrapped tightly with a cord above the elbow to prevent loss of blood at the elbow, a minie ball having gone through it at the joint and crushed all the bones.

"On arrival at the church I found an operating table in the entry, with the double folding doors open for light during the operations then going on, for the battle had opened about 10 o'clock and wounded men for hours had been making their way to the rear of the church.

"Awaiting my turn for examination and treatment, I went into an empty pew on the left-hand side of the church, the west side and the third or fourth pew from the street, suffering at the time greatly, unbuckled my sword scabbard and my revolver, asked some men to tear the pew-door off its hinges and place it crosswise on the back and front of the pew. On this I placed my swollen arm and got some relief from the intense pain; I then called for some whiskey and got and swallowed the largest drink I ever took in my life.

"About six o'clock an assistant to the general surgeons who were operating at the table came to me announcing it was my turn. I went to the table and got onto it with my head towards the west. I took some chloroform but not enough, for I distinctly remember having said, 'Oh, don't saw the bone until I have had more chloroform!' What I next remember was my saying, 'You took off my arm, did you, Doctor? I thought you were only going to examine and dress it; well, when we next march through

Maryland I will have to salute with my left hand.' I then swung off the table, feet first, and was told to seek a place in the pulpit to lie down, which I attempted to do, stepping carefully among the hundreds of soldiers who were lying in the aisles and blocked my way. On arriving at the pulpit I found the floor of it filled with wounded men, as had been the aisles. Spying the gallery at the other end of the church, I worked my way back to the operating table and ascended the stairs to the gallery, which as I thought, was empty. I found a 'soft' board near the railing of the gallery and there lay down with my head towards the west and not far from the organ . . . ."

Col. Huidekoper remained in the gallery while the church was captured in the Confederate advance. He resumes:

"Next day, the 2nd, in the afternoon, General Ewell and several of his staff officers came up into the gallery for observation from the cupola of the church. As the General had only one leg, the other having been lost in 1862, he was unable to go up the ladder to the roof and sat down on the bench not three feet from me. His aides called down to the General from time to time, 'Things are going splendidly; we are driving them back and gaining everywhere.' This was as to the battle on the afternoon of the 2nd, in which Sickles played so important a part. As General Ewell sat near me I had an opportunity to study his features and the gorgeous gold lace which adorned the sleeves and collar and front of his gray coat.

"About this time a Miss Myers and a younger girl came to me and asked whether or not I was badly wounded and wanted anything. In answer I threw back the blanket that covered me and said that I had had nothing to eat since daylight the morning of the 1st and did want a bite. They went away but returned in ten minutes from their

homes near-by and gave me a glass of home-made wine
and one cracker, which Miss Myers had to carry hidden
under her shawl lest she might encounter some hungry
rebel. Later in the day the girls came for me and I walked
with them a hundred feet to the house of Squire Myers,
where I was fed and given a bed until about the 9th of
July, when I took a car for Baltimore, not a day-coach,
but a freight-car that had come to Gettysburg with ice
for the wounded, with the floor still damp. We, Major
Chamberlin of my regiment and I, lay on the damp floor
with little straw under us and suffered much from the
jolting during the twelve hours to Baltimore over a
wretched roadbed. . . . "

FIELD AND GENERAL HOSPITALS

During the battle eight corps hospitals were
set up on the field, convenient to the positions
of the various corps. A general hospital, to
which those whose wounds required long attention were transferred as soon as possible, was
established in a beautiful wood on the York
Pike 1¾ miles from Gettysburg. It was named
for Surgeon Jonathan Letterman, Medical Director of the Army of the Potomac. The problem
which confronted the medical staff may be understood from the following extracts from the reports of inspectors.

"I arrived at Gettysburg about 7 P.M., on July 8th,
and in consequence of some irregularity or delay in the
railroad trains, there were about 2,000 slightly wounded
men collected at a point a mile from town, where the trains

Airplane View of the National Cemetery, with its curving rows
of headstones

National Monument. On the site of this National Monument stood
the platform from which Abraham Lincoln delivered his immortal
address on November 19, 1863. (See page 157)

had stopped, without food, shelter, or attendance for the night. Fortunately, through the agents of the Sanitary Commission, these men were all fed, and some 300 sheltered that night. No system had as yet been adopted for the transportation of the wounded. . . .

"The railroad authorities were perplexed and deficient in motive power and rolling stock. The telegraph wires were down, and the obstruction to transportation seemed insurmountable until General Haupt arrived and assumed military control of the road to Hanover Junction. We then experienced no further delays till the 18th, when an important bridge on the road to Harrisburg gave way under a cattle train, thus diverting, for the following five days, the trains that were intended for New York to Baltimore and York, Pa."—REPORT OF MEDICAL INSPECTOR EDWARD P. VOLLUM, U. S. A.

"I arrived at Gettysburg on the morning of the 10th of July, forty hours later than I had hoped to do, in consequence of the irregularities and interruptions on the railways leading to that place. Medical Inspector Vollum reached Gettysburg some two or three days in advance of me, and immediately on his arrival made arrangements for sending away such of the wounded as were in a condition to be moved in ambulances or on the railroad. Lieutenant-Colonel Vollum had the immediate charge of forwarding the wounded to the general hospitals designated by Surgeon-General William A. Hammond. In this he was assisted by Dr. Osborne, of the Army of the Potomac.

"The number of medical officers detailed by Medical Director Letterman to remain with the wounded was thought to be sufficient, and probably might have been had not thousands of the enemy's wounded been thrown unexpectedly on our hands. For some days after the battle, many of the Rebel wounded were in a most deplorable condition, being without shelter of any sort, and with

an insufficient number of medical officers and nurses of their own army.

"Every effort was made to alleviate the sufferings of these unfortunate men, and as soon as it was possible they were placed under cover or sent away to some general hospital.

"Our wounded, with some few exceptions, were sheltered within a day or two after the battle, and made as comfortable as circumstances would permit. The scarcity of straw for bedding was seriously felt, and it was not until eight or ten days after the conflict that a sufficient quantity could be obtained. As far as my observation extends, the medical directors of the army, and the citizen surgeons who were employed during the emergency, discharged their arduous duties with fidelity and ability. . . .

"Up to the 25th instant (the day I left Gettysburg), 15,875 of the wounded had been sent away, and since that time 250 more have been forwarded, amounting in all to 16,125, leaving still at Gettysburg about 3,500, 3,000 of whom, it is believed, are not in condition to be moved at present. Those who are obliged to remain will be quartered in a large field hospital established at a suitable place near the town, where I hope they will have all the comfort and receive all the attention and kindness to which they are so justly entitled.

"I cannot close this report without acknowledging the immense aid afforded by the Sanitary and Christian Commissions. The promptness, energy, and great kindness uniformly exhibited by these benevolent associations doubtless helped to save the lives of many, and gladdened the hearts of thousands, who, with their friends scattered throughout the land, will hold their good and noble deeds in grateful remembrance."—REPORTS OF MEDICAL IN-SPECTOR JOHN M. CUYLER, U. S. A.

CHAPTER XIII

THE SOLDIERS' NATIONAL CEMETERY

OF THE eighty-three cemeteries in the United States which are dedicated exclusively to the burial of soldiers, that at Gettysburg was the first.

A few days after the battle, Governor A. G. Curtin, of Pennsylvania, solicitous for the welfare of the soldiers, came to Gettysburg and appointed David Wills, a leading attorney, to act as his agent in the work of establishing a cemetery. Correspondence with the governors of other States was begun. Grounds were selected by Mr. Wills, and by the direction of Governor Curtin purchased for the State of Pennsylvania, to provide a burial-place for soldiers who fell in the battle.

Lots in the cemetery were tendered without cost to each State having dead upon the field. The expense of removing the bodies, laying out, ornamenting and enclosing the grounds, building a lodge for the keeper, and erecting a suitable monument to the memory of the dead, was to be borne by the several States, assessed in proportion to their population.

The seventeen acres of land which were purchased lie on Cemetery Hill adjoining the

Citizens' Cemetery, at the apex of what had been the triangular battle-line of the Union Army, and an important tactical position on July 2nd and 3rd. At the time of the battle this land was a cornfield, divided by stone fences which were used to great advantage by the infantry of the Union Army. The most elevated portions had been points of vantage for many batteries of artillery.

The land was surrounded on the west, east, and north by a substantial, well-built wall of native granite, topped by a heavy dressed coping. A division fence of iron was erected between the Soldiers' National Cemetery and the Citizens' Cemetery.

The plans and designs for the laying out of the cemetery were prepared by William Saunders, an able landscape gardener of the Department of Agriculture, Washington, D. C. A semicircular plan for the arrangement of the graves was adopted. The ground allotted to each State converges upon a central point. The size of each plot was determined by the number of graves belonging to each State. The bodies were placed side by side in parallel trenches with a space of twelve feet to each parallel and with a grass path between the rows of graves. The outer section is lettered A, and so on in alphabetical order. Two feet of space was allowed to each body, and a person standing in

the center of the semi-circle and facing the circumference reads the names from left to right. The bodies are laid with the heads towards the center. The headstones are uniform in size and contain the name, regiment and company of each soldier so far as it was possible to obtain them. Another lot was set apart for the soldiers of the Regular Army. The graves of the unknown dead are located at each end of the semi-circle.

On the 27th of October, 1863, the work of exhumation was begun under the supervision of Samuel Weaver, a citizen of Gettysburg. It was completed on March 18th, 1864. The number of bodies exhumed and interred in the cemetery was 3,512, including 158 taken up by the authorities of Boston. Of the total number, 979 were unknown. Later other bodies were discovered and added, and the total interred was 3,734. Many other Union dead were sent to their family burial places. The Confederate bodies remained in the original trenches until 1870–73, when 3,320 were transferred to southern cemeteries.

The central point of the semi-circle from which Lincoln delivered his address is now occupied by the National Monument, one of the finest on the field. It is 60 feet in height; the pedestal, 25 feet square at the base, is crowned by a colossal statue representing the Genius of Lib-

erty. Projecting from the angles are four buttresses, each supporting an allegorical statue.

From the point where this monument stands, a magnificent view is presented to the beholder. Sloping gradually toward the north and the west, the entire cemetery is spread out as a beautiful panorama, showing on a carpet of green the semi-circle of graves, the driveways lined with rows of splendid maples, spruces, birches, magnolias, and many other trees, as well as many clumps of shrubbery filling the intervals between. A view from this point as the sun sinks behind the distant range of the South Mountain is one long to be remembered.

Standing at the upper end of the cemetery is a lesser monument in the form of an exedra, the center of which contains a bust of Lincoln. Two panels, one to the left, the other to the right, contain inscriptions; one giving David Wills' letter of invitation to President Lincoln to attend the exercises on November 19th, 1863; the other, Lincoln's immortal address.

Opposite this monument is the Rostrum from which the memorial addresses are now delivered. The first memorial exercise was held on May 30th, 1868, establishing a custom continued until this day. Among the speakers of recent years, either in the cemetery or on adjoining sections of the Park, have been Presidents Roosevelt, Taft, Wilson, Coolidge, and Hoover.

CHAPTER XIV

THE CONFEDERATE WOUNDED DURING THE RETREAT

GENERAL LEE ordered Dr. Guild, his Medical Director, to see that all the wounded who could bear the journey were carried back in the empty wagons and ambulances. What this journey would mean to many no one seemed to foresee. General Imboden, who had charge of this train on which the wounded were moved, gives the following description in "Battles and Leaders":

"Shortly after noon on the 4th, the very windows of heaven seemed to have opened. The rain fell in blinding sheets, the meadows were soon overflowed, and fences gave way before the raging streams. During the storm, wagons, ambulances, and artillery carriages by hundreds—nay, by thousands—were assembling in the fields along the road from Gettysburg to Cashtown in one confused and apparently inextricable mass. As the afternoon wore on, there was no abatement in the storm. Canvas was no protection against its fury, and the wounded men lying upon the naked boards of the wagon-bodies were drenched, horses and mules were blinded and maddened by the wind and water, and became almost unmanageable."

Imboden also gives the following harrowing description:

"After dark I set out from Cashtown to gain the

head of the column during the night. My orders had been peremptory that there should be no halt for any cause whatever. If an accident should happen to any vehicle, it was immediately to be put out of the road and abandoned. The column moved rapidly, considering the rough roads and the darkness, and from almost every wagon issued heart-rending wails of agony. For four hours I hurried forward on my way to the front, and in all that time I was never out of hearing of the groans and cries of the wounded and dying. Scarcely one in a hundred had received adequate surgical aid, owing to the demands on the hard-working surgeons from still worse cases which had been left behind. Many of the wounded in the wagons had been without food for 36 hours. Their torn and bloody clothing, matted and hardened, was rasping the tender, inflamed, and still oozing wounds. Very few of the wagons had even a layer of straw in them, and all were without springs. The road was rough and rocky from the heavy washings of the preceding day. The jolting was enough to have killed strong men if long exposed to it.

"From nearly every wagon, as the teams trotted on urged by whip and shout, came such cries and shrieks as these:

'Oh God! Why can't I die!'
'My God! Will no one have mercy and kill me!'
'Stop! Oh! for God's sake stop just for one minute; take me out and leave me to die by the roadside.'
'I am dying! I am dying! My poor wife, my dear children! What will become of you?'

"No help could be rendered to any of the sufferers. No heed could be given to any of their appeals. Mercy and duty to the many forbade the loss of a moment in the vain effort then and there to comply with the prayers of the few. On! On! We *must* move on. The storm

continued, and the darkness was appalling. There was no time to fill a canteen of water for a dying man, for, except the drivers and the guards, all were wounded and utterly helpless in that vast procession of misery."

THE BIVOUAC OF THE DEAD

THEODORE O'HARA

The muffled drum's sad roll has beat
　　The soldier's last tattoo;
No more on life's parade shall meet
　　That brave and fallen few.
On fame's eternal camping-ground
　　Their silent tents are spread,
And glory guards with solemn round,
　　The bivouac of the dead.

No rumor of the foe's advance
　　Now swells upon the wind;
No troubled thought at midnight haunts
　　Of loved ones left behind;
No vision of the morrow's strife
　　The warror's dream alarms;
No braying horn nor screaming fife
　　At dawn shall call to arms.
　　. . . . .
Rest on, embalmed and sainted dead,
　　Dear as the blood you gave;
No impious footsteps here shall tread
　　The herbage of your grave;
Nor shall your glory be forgot
　　While fame her record keeps
Or honor points the hallowed spot
　　Where valor proudly sleeps.
　　. . . . .

ORGANIZATION OF THE ARMY OF THE POTOMAC

General George G. Meade

First Corps
John F. Reynolds, Major General
John Newton, Major General

Divisions	*Brigades*
1. James S. Wadsworth Brigadier General	1. Solomon Meredith, Brig. Gen. 2. Lysander Cutler, Brig. Gen.
2. John C. Robinson Brigadier General	1. Gabriel R. Paul, Brig. Gen. 2. Henry Baxter, Brig. Gen.
3. Abner Doubleday Major General	1. Thomas Rowley, Brig. Gen. 2. Roy Stone, Col. 3. George J. Stannard, Brig. Gen.

Second Corps
Winfield S. Hancock, Major General

Divisions	*Brigades*
1. John C. Caldwell Brigadier General	1. Edward E. Cross, Col. 2. Patrick Kelly, Col. 3. Samuel K. Zook, Brig. Gen. 4. John R. Brooke, Col.
2. John Gibbon Brigadier General	1. William Harrow, Brig. Gen. 2. Alexander Webb, Brig. Gen. 3. Norman J. Hall, Col.
3. Alexander Hays Brigadier General	1. Samuel S. Carroll, Col. 2. Thomas A. Smyth, Col. 3. George L. Willard, Col.

Third Corps
Daniel E. Sickles, Major General

Divisions	*Brigades*
1. David D. Birney Major General	1. Charles K. Graham, Brig. Gen. 2. J. H. Hobart Ward, Brig. Gen. 3. Regis de Trobriand, Col.
2. Andrew A. Humphreys Brigadier General	1. Joseph B. Carr, Brig. Gen. 2. Wm. R. Brewster, Col. 3. George C. Burling, Col.

Fifth Corps
George Sykes, Major General

Divisions	Brigades
1. James Barnes Brigadier General	1. William S. Tilton, Col. 2. Jacob B. Sweitzer, Col. 3. Strong Vincent, Col.

2. George Sykes
    Major General
    Romeyn B. Ayres
    Brigadier General
	1. Hannibal Day, Col.
	2. Sidney Burbank, Col.
	3. Stephen Weed, Brig. Gen.

3. Samuel W. Crawford Brigadier General	1. William McCandless, Col. 2. Joseph W. Fisher, Col.

Sixth Corps
John Sedgwick, Major General

Divisions	Brigades
1. Horatio G. Wright Brigadier General	1. Alfred T. A. Torbert, Brig. Gen. 2. Joseph J. Bartlett, Brig. Gen. 3. David A. Russell, Brig. Gen.
2. Albion P. Howe Brigadier General	1. Lewis A. Grant, Col. 2. Thomas H. Neill, Brig. Gen.

3. John Newton
    Major General
    Frank Wheaton
    Brigadier General
	1. Alexander Shaler, Brig. Gen.
	2. Henry L. Eustis, Col.
	3. Frank Wheaton, Brig. Gen.

Eleventh Corps
Oliver O. Howard, Major General

Divisions	Brigades
1. Francis C. Barlow Brigadier General	1. Leopold von Gilsa, Col. 2. Adelbert Ames, Brig. Gen.
2. Adolph von Steinwehr Brigadier General	1. Charles Coster, Col. 2. Orlando Smith, Col.
3. Carl Schurz Major General	1. Alexander Schimmelfennig, Brig. Gen. 2. W. Krzyzanowski, Col.

GETTYSBURG

Twelfth Corps
Henry W. Slocum, Major General

Divisions	Brigades
1. Alpheus S. Williams Brigadier General	1. Archibald L. McDougal, Col. 2. Henry H. Lockwood, Brig. Gen. 3. Thomas H. Huger, Brig. Gen.
2. John W. Geary Brigadier General	1. Charles Candy, Col. 2. George A. Cobham, Col. 3. George S. Greene, Brig. Gen.

Cavalry
Alfred Pleasanton, Major General

Divisions	Brigades
1. John Buford Brigadier General	1. William Gamble, Col. 2. Thomas C. Devin, Col. 3. Wesley Merritt, Brig. Gen.
2. David McM. Gregg Brigadier General	1. John B. McIntosh, Col. 2. Pennock Ruey, Col. 3. J. Irvin Gregg, Col.
3. Judson Kilpatrick Brigadier General	1. Elon J. Farnsworth, Brig. Gen. 2. George A. Custer, Brig. Gen.

Chief of Artillery, Brigadier-General Henry J. Hunt
Number of guns belonging to the Artillery, 362
Number of guns at Gettysburg, 354

ORGANIZATION OF THE ARMY OF NORTHERN VIRGINIA

General Robert E. Lee

First Corps
James E. Longstreet, Lieutenant General

Divisions	*Brigades*
1. Lafayette McLaws Major General	1. John B. Kershaw, Brig. Gen. 2. William Barksdale, Brig. Gen. 3. Paul J. Semmes, Brig. Gen. 4. William T. Wofford, Brig. Gen.
2. George E. Pickett Major General	1. Richard B. Garnett, Brig. Gen. 2. James L. Kemper, Brig. Gen. 3. Lewis A. Armistead, Brig. Gen.
3. John B. Hood Major General	1. Evander Law, Brig. Gen. 2. Jerome B. Robertson, Brig. Gen. 3. George T. Anderson, Brig. Gen. 4. Henry L. Benning, Brig. Gen.

Second Corps
Richard S. Ewell, Lieutenant General

Divisions	*Brigades*
1. Jubal A. Early Major General	1. Harry T. Hays, Brig. Gen. 2. Robert F. Hoke (Isaac E. Avery), Brig. Gen. 3. William Smith, Brig. Gen. 4. John B. Gordon, Brig. Gen.
2. Edward Johnson Major General	1. George H. Steuart, Brig. Gen. 2. James A. Walker, Brig. Gen. 3. Francis T. Nicholls (J. M. Williams), Brig. Gen. 4. John M. Jones, Brig. Gen.
3. Robert E. Rodes Major General	1. Junius Daniel, Brig. Gen. 2. Alfred Iverson, Brig. Gen. 3. George Doles, Brig. Gen. 4. Stephen D. Ramseur, Brig. Gen. 5. Edward A. O'Neil, Brig. Gen.

Third Corps
Ambrose P. Hill, Lieutenant General

Divisions	*Brigades*
1. Richard H. Anderson Major General	1. Cadmus M. Wilcox, Brig. Gen. 2. Ambrose R. Wright, Brig. Gen. 3. William Mahone, Brig. Gen. 4. Edward A. Perry (David Lang), Brig. Gen. 5. Garnet Posey, Brig. Gen.
2. Henry Heth Major General	1. James J. Pettigrew, Brig. Gen. 2. John M. Brockenbrough, Col. 3. James J. Archer, Brig. Gen. 4. Joseph R. Davis, Brig. Gen.
3. William D. Pender Major General	1. James H. Lane, Brig. Gen. 2. Edward L. Thomas, Brig. Gen. 3. Alfred M. Scales, Brig. Gen. 4. Samuel McGowan (Abner Perrin), Brig. Gen.
4. James E. B. Stuart Major General (Cavalry)	1. Wade Hampton, Brig. Gen. 2. Beverly H. Robertson, Brig. Gen. 3. Fitzhugh Lee, Brig. Gen. 4. Wm. H. F. Lee (John R. Chambliss), Brig. Gen. 5. William E. Jones, Brig. Gen.
Valley District and Department of Western Virginia (Cavalry and mounted Infantry).	1. Albert G. Jenkins, Brig. Gen. 2. John D. Imboden, Brig. Gen.

Chief of Artillery, William N. Pendleton
Number of guns, 272